THE BUSINESS OF WHO

ROSS ASDOURIAN

For my Family.
For giving me the freedom to explore the many stories, in flesh and in ritual, all this crazy planet has to offer.

CHAPTER 1

LEMONADE

THE UNITED STATES currently hosts at least 30.2 million registered small businesses. This means that approximately one in every eleven people owns one. That doesn't even count the unofficial lemonade stands running as a cash operation. So, in this sea of competition, how on Earth do you make yourself stand out? Numerous academic institutions across the nation have full courses and degrees to formulate an answer to this question, but there's a critical part of the curriculum that's frequently left out.

Most businesses construct a plan that encapsulates their company description, market analysis, sales strategy, financial projection, and identity. This book will drill down into the last of these components. As well as being the most personal of the group, identity also forms the bedrock of your marketing, purpose, and community. Investing the time to introspectively examine who you are and who you aspire to be creates a robust foundation for an enduring empire, from unit storage to unicorn.

Our first goal is to understand what storytelling is according to the fundamentals. Then, we will look at how to tell *your* story, including the pitfalls and landmines that could send you to the gulag. And finally, we're going to connect how your story relates to your business and the community you create. It's a lot of information, but no less than you're taking in every day. Consumers process millions of data points every day, leading to habitual, unconscious consumer behavior. This automatic assimilation of information influences our decisions, our social preferences, the brands we identify with, and the brands that we feel we best embody. With that in mind, let's start with the basics.

Who Am I?

An excellent question. Depending on who you ask, there may be some discrepancies between who I am and who I claim to be. As we will explore in the chapter titled "The Biggest 4 Questions of Your Life," answering this question is just a fragment of the puzzle. But for now, let me offer you a conventional response. My name is Ross Asdourian. I was born in Miami but think of myself as a New Yorker due to my tendency to shout at automobiles. I have spent over a decade working as a video producer at NBC News, Red Bull Media House, and a few credits at Facebook Watch in between years of commercial production. Everywhere I go, I'm telling someone else's story and using the full understanding of my own story to get the talent there. My other income streams include an Amazon shop and as another book, a somewhat unorthodox autobiography revolving around a rather unfortunate accident. There was also that time I designed a lipstick line for proud Puerto Ricans, but that's another book. You'll discover more about me, such as my childhood dream job, as we delve deeper into this journey.

Why Am I Writing This?

Over a few summers at the University of Penn, I had the privilege of delivering guest lectures at the Wharton School of Business. My good friend (and inexhaustible benefactor) Tina Wells invited me to her summer class to provide a refreshing deviation from the conventional curriculum. Preparing for my lecture, "Storytelling in Business and Marketing," compelled me to answer three fundamental questions:

What do I know?
How have I acquired this knowledge?
How can I effectively disseminate this knowledge?

Over time, we each hone skills that gradually become second nature. Talent morphs into skill. Skill evolves into a profession. The profession becomes automated. Throughout my life, I have been weaving stories, sometimes my own, sometimes others', and frequently blending others' stories into a brand narrative. When Tina requested my lecture, I grappled with the specter of imposter syndrome. How do I execute this? How do I even know how to do this? A defined process existed, and my lecture allowed me to refine it into a teachable series. After delivering this lecture multiple times, I've finally reached a place where I can share it with entrepreneurs encountering distinct challenges.

Who Are You?

This question has myriad answers, but let's begin with entrepreneur, hustler, marketer, advertiser, perpetual student, business owner, or a future iteration of any of these. Your business education and experience have furnished you with a robust toolset, encompassing areas such as markets, customers, finances, operations, communications, information technologies, policies, and strategies. Despite its comprehensiveness, it omits the most critical component. 'Who you are' is a question we will examine in profound depth in the ensuing chapters. At its core, it acknowledges that business transcends mere spreadsheets and profit lines.

The Goal

The aim of this book is to comprehend the notion of 'story' as it pertains to you, your business, and the reality you shape. With this understanding, the book will equip you with the capacity to articulate your narrative either directly or through your brand identity. We will decipher the mechanics and learn to circumvent the pitfalls of preconditioning. Our brains process far more data than we realize, often guiding our decisions and preferences unconsciously. When you comprehend the essence of a story, both in the context of street wisdom and academic knowledge, you will be able to recognize your own.

Takeaways

You will gain an understanding of your role within the framework of your work. Your business will transform from a purely operational entity into a living, breathing organism with distinct characteristics. These attributes all adhere to a value system you should comprehend at an early stage. This foundational understanding will become your blueprint for the elusive "A" word – authenticity.

This book is designed to equip you with the tools to uncover your story and construct its future. Each chapter presents concepts explored in the original Wharton lecture series, interspersed with philosophical examples from the worlds of business and entertainment. Additionally, we'll weave in interviews from successful entrepreneurs who have achieved their success without the aid of celebrity. With this in mind, let's embark on this journey.

WHY DO YOU DO WHAT YOU DO? How did you get to where you are?

A few years ago, I found myself in the halls of the Wharton Business School. Out of place and out of time, I hurried through the brick campus to find a group of 60 students. Each of them were waiting for me, a producer at Red Bull Media House at the time, to give a lecture. It wasn't the first instance of feeling like a foreigner. When I was 19 years old, I had my first internship at Sony in Santa Monica. The entire week prior to my first day was spent on deciding what to wear. Do I dress for the job I want (respected employee)? Or do I dress for the job I've got (unpaid intern)? In an attempt to be cool yet still show respect, I tucked my blue flannel into skinnier-than-me jeans and black Converse. Oh, and a tie. My tucked in flannel button down in the LA heat with a tie. All of this is to say, I was an idiot. I knew nothing. I had a whiny pop punk band in high school and thought I could fake my worth at a top record company. Maybe you've felt the nerves of walking into a new place. Maybe you've felt like you don't belong just like me on that day. Hopefully, you didn't dress like me, though, especially on that day.

As I stepped through the welcoming automatic doors of Epic Records, a Sony music label, the air conditioning attempted to re-solidify my carefully applied hair gel. I wore a smile that was both undeniably huge and clearly nervous.

Brian Murphy, my soon-to-be boss, awaited my arrival. Towering over me by a foot and filling the hallway with his imposing build, Brian, a former football player at Colorado University and the newly-minted director of digital marketing, called out my name with a sense of authority that was both startling and thrilling.

"Ross," his deep voice echoed through the hall, "Welcome to the shit show, buddy."

At this point in my life, cursing still came as a shock. I was far away from the suburbs of Central Florida, and I had to be cool. As our hands met in a firm handshake, I squeezed with every bit of strength my lean frame could muster, hoping to impart a sense of conviction and courage. This, after all, was a handshake with a former linebacker. Brian, never missing a beat, arched a brow and fixed me with a piercing gaze.

"So. Why the hell did you choose this place?" He asked, a playful grin adorning his features. Despite the countless techniques, tips, and rehearsed responses racing through my mind, I found myself offering a response that was far from genuine. I had applied to no less than 15 internships and this was one of the two I'd be working. The other, as a disposable coffee fetcher at KROQ's Kevin and Bean in the Morning Show, would be starting the following week during the "not-worth-it" shift from 5-8:30am.

"I've always wanted to work at a place like Sony, and I'm excited to learn more about the business." At that moment, I realized how far from the truth my answer had strayed. The truth was that I didn't actually have a good answer. "This is the one I got," wouldn't exactly set me up for success, even if it was partially true. I hadn't done the work to understand what had led me there, and why this label represented an extension of who I was. As entrepreneurs and professionals in business, we have to seek out the why and the what in our connections if anyone is supposed to care. For years, I was in pursuit of the perfect professional response, not realizing that the real answer lay inside of my lived experiences.

This book uses real stories. The stories that matter are often the ones that build genuine connections. They are, after all, the cornerstone of every successful venture. But first, let's go to the beginning and define what a good story is, and the intricate role it plays in the world of an entrepreneur.

CHAPTER 2

THE BACKSTORY OF GOOD STORY

WHY THE TALE is Essential
to the Entrepreneur's Condition

If you're not a natural storyteller, you may already be feeling a certain way toward this book. Why can't products and price lists on their own suffice? The answer lies in our preposterously complex human brains, and the way they are wired to receive information through narrative. Even left-brainers who love nothing more than unprocessed datasets and cold hard calculus retain some primordial penchant for a plot. As Aswath Damodaran, a New York University professor who teaches equity valuation, admits: "one of the most important lessons I have learned is that a valuation that is not backed up by a story is both soulless and untrustworthy and that we remember stories better than spreadsheets."[1] Brené Brown, University of Houston professor and TED Talk extraordinaire, simplifies the analogy: "maybe stories are just data with a soul."[2]

The concept of 'soul' in matters of business and finance is

increasingly salient as entrepreneurs battle to cut through screeds of competing products and services in the market. As self-employment rises, with its flexible working hours and uncapped earning potential, the marketplace has become flooded with start-ups, social media influencers, life coaches, and 'personality brand' businesses. Don't be disheartened by the size of the pool. It's flooded, yes, but inflate your entrepreneurial life vest and you'll quickly rise to the top. Stories are your water wings and, in today's business world, they're the difference between sink and swim.

Right, but *Good* Story

In my lectures, I often emphasize that at the core of every compelling story lie three components: character, conflict, and resolution. However, during lecture the students' instinct is to find fault frantically and search for holes. Someone's counter-argument inevitably reaches their mouth before having a proper trial-by-brain. A hand shoots up and after a nod of permission, words shoot out.

"I went to the store and bought groceries. That's a story, isn't it?" Dax, a young man, enters the chat. A few classmates laugh because, to a certain extent, he's got a point.

"Why would you consider this a story?" I ask. The trick to teaching, so I'm told, isn't to lead with the answer.

"Well, I mean, it's a story because I just told it to you, and there's no conflict. But that's still a story." My lips purse throughout my pondering as silence thickens the room. A full second of dead air goes by.

When I was in college, the only class I'd speak up in was Film Studies. I failed every quiz because reading in film class went against my religion. Instead, I'd always participate in hopes the professor would let the quiz thing slide. He didn't. Instead, he told me to drop the class before midterms so the F wouldn't bring down my GPA. Dax's inquisition felt like he was sent there as payback for the times I was the pesky student.

"Well?" I ask the class without actually asking a question. Three seconds of dead air go by, further crippling the idea of staying silent.

"I mean, yeah I think it's a story but," another classmate lets out, "it's a not a *good* story." The classroom shakes a laugh out of their buttoned-up business attire. The business kids started to loosen up.

⊏━━⊐

A STORY IS... well, a *good* story is a specific experience that some people (...animals or objects) relate (or react) to in a given context. As any marketer will attest in the name of job security, building it does not mean they will come. Having a good story means creating an emotional connection or reaction of any magnitude. A viewer doesn't have to cry to feel sad, and people certainly don't laugh at everything that's funny. If a good story is an emotional experience, then consumers need another force to sift through the plethora of options. There's another add on to consider.

We are attracted to stories that genuinely reflect who we are and what we desire. Traditionally, advertisers tell us what we want by showing us. Mass market companies implant an image of who we should want to be and let it germinate. Now that consumers have more control, or at least that perception, they seek media and merchandise that reinforce who they are. In a sense, using reflective stories to form communities. Buzzfeed, the entertainment news site that has birthed many viral stories of the past decade, uses reflective story.

When I worked for the NBC NewsGroup, I listened to

Buzzfeed CEO Jonah Peretti speak about this approach. Articles rely on our identity and interests to gain our attention, and their site traffic heavily depends on listicles. At the talk, he was quick to point out that this, along with a team of data scientists, gives you a reason to share their content. Their articles include "20 Florida Things Only People Who Grew Up There Will Understand,"[3] "19 Weird Things That Are So, So Ohio,"[4] or "22 Hilariously Awkward Signs from India." [5] All of these articles use location and culture, and they are not alone. With 65% of the viral articles being lists, Buzzfeed relies on these identities for their record-setting traffic. Buzzfeed looks for content that an audience can relate to, including favorite shows, food, books, shoes, and movies.

⊏⊐

"Okay, okay," I calmly brush over the giggling class, "What happens if you give me more details about your grocery encounter?" The pupil gets a second chance.

"Okay. Umm, let's see," Dax says, thinking out loud. "Once upon a time..."

"Yes, I like this, go on."

"I went to the grocery store and grabbed some cool ranch snack mix."

"Why cool ranch snack mix?" I prod. Dax pauses before letting out the only answer his adolescence allows.

"Because I'm stoned" The class bursts out laughing.

"Okay, very good. So, to be clear, you are stoned," I acknowledge.

"So when I get to the register to pay, I realize I don't have my wallet," he continues to giggle. As though the class is in on it, everyone plays along in the chorus.

"Because you are stoned..."

"Yes," he giggles. "But I always keep five dollars cash in my pants just in case, so I was able to pay for the snacks." By now, we are all enjoying this unprofessional story.

"Now wait," I pause, "Is that true?" The student rummages, moving in his chair so he can dig into his tight little pockets. Without another blink, he pulls out two dollars in cash.

"Wait. Are you high right now?!" I joke with Dax. He had given the class a gift.

If you do not have character, conflict, and resolution, you only have a memory. That is the difference between going to the store and going to the store stoned. Amidst the investor meetings, product development, marketing research, and sales pitches that entrepreneurs often find themselves navigating, a critical task emerges - the art of captivating the listener's attention. Underscoring the importance of story to an entrepreneur is to doom the longevity of their intellectual property. Since we're talking about intellect, let's dive a little further into history and neuroscience.

Once Upon a Time

The art of storytelling is subjective and incredibly varied – adapting to the tools of its time. Ancient cave etchings, modern fairy tale that shape our earliest thoughts, and even 28-character Twitter (or "X") rants capturing the short attention spans of the modern world, storytelling has woven its influence throughout history. It possesses the unique power of not only informing but also manipulating those around us, preserving our cultures and guiding us for the future.

Narratives are the universal language to communicate with each other. Think about it – on the first day of school, we do not hand children spreadsheets and datasets; but immerse them in the magical world of tales to light up their imaginations. As kids, we're taught the importance of friendship through the pantless, honey-mad bear *Winnie the Pooh*, and all the merchandise that came with him (fun fact: Winnie was actually named after a female bear[6]). *The Boy Who Cried Wolf* struck fear in our hearts about the consequences of lying. In the classroom, teachers wielded stories to breathe life into their lessons, turning the driest subjects into captivating adventures. At our weddings, inflated stories of love and romance without struggle take center stage. When we die, people stand next to our corpse and share anecdotes capturing the essence of our lives. Strange but fascinating, right? Morbid or not, business is one of life's more serious spheres, but that does not absolve it from the detailed pages of history.

Human beings have been spinning yarns as a means of effective communication for tens of thousands of years, back to when the oldest cave paintings are dated. Cave dwellers drew animals on their walls to teach skills and document life. Today we post puppy videos to our Facebook walls – also to document life – and to secure the easiest 'likes' of our time. Time goes on, but storytelling endures. Throughout history, we've mastered the art of selling, telling, manipulating, loving, grieving, warring, peace-making, worshiping , and even hallucinating – all through the medium of story. However, our predilection for the parable is not only a cultural thing. Storytelling is hardwired into our psychology.

Remember That (It's All in Your Head)

Generally speaking, any verbal information we receive lights up the language-processing parts of our brain. We take it in, extract meaning from what are ostensibly grunts and slurs, and then proceed to forget it ten minutes later. When we hear a *story*, on the other hand, more parts of our brain fire up and take part in the receiving of information. Back in 2006, Spanish researchers published findings that demonstrated just how impactful stories are on our minds. They asked participants to read words associated with smells, like "coffee" and "cinnamon" and found that their primary olfactory cortex lit up – the part of the brain charged with processing smell and taste.[7] The participants' brains didn't need to taste or smell coffee or cinnamon to engage with the *idea* of those things. The words alone tap into our emotional connection with food and bring them to life.

Telling stories infused with emotion, taste, and smell, captures attention in a way pure data simply cannot. I'm going to describe a party to you in general terms:

Yesterday, I went to Chris's house for his birthday. We played games, hung with friends, and enjoyed a nice Summer day in his yard.

You can see it, right? At least, enough of it to know it qualifies as a party (people, games, weather). If I tell it again, this time with more of a narrative, it can light up other parts of your brain – making the information more relatable, enjoyable, and memorable. This version takes aim at more parts of the brain – those dealing with smell and sight and taste and memory. These right-side parts of the brain are those that the all-powerful neocortex originally grew from. This explains why our emotional centers have so much influence over our communication preferences and decision-making.

Yesterday, I went to Chris's house for his birthday, and he does not take birthday parties lightly! He hosted everyone at his historic, two-story house out in the suburbs, and the sunny weather only made it more picturesque. His girlfriend, a volleyball player from Texas, made her famous yellow cornbread. Everyone could smell it airing out from the open kitchen windows, and I'm pretty sure some people started salivating. About half-way through the party, a karaoke DJ showed up and plugged his gear in. With everyone well aware of what was about to happen, we flocked to the coolers to top up our drinks. We sang a lot of 90s pop and caught up with some old friends before finally headed home for dinner.

Descriptive stories like this one prompt a part of the brain called the insula to kick in. Descriptive stories give an audience touch points to relate and find parallels to their memories. Storytelling, then, creates connections in a way that pure data cannot.

The CEO Chronicles

It's no surprise that marketers use storytelling to sell products and services. At its heart, good marketing is, and has always been, about creating an arc. However, this principle should extend beyond your marketing team. Stories work like a charm to establish a business, legitimize it, grow it, and see it through the tough times. Stories trump authority when it comes to leadership. They beat slogans and company principles as team motivators. The most innovative firms put storytelling in the foundation. The trouble is when a founder or CEO opts to manufacture one. An example of a CEO manufacturing a false narrative is Elizabeth Holmes, the founder and former CEO of Theranos, a company that claimed to revolutionize blood testing with a device that could perform hundreds of tests with a single drop of blood. Holmes was hailed as a visionary and a self-made billionaire, but it turned out that her device was unreliable, inaccurate, and fraudulent. She lied to investors, regulators, customers, and the public about the capabilities and performance of her device, and concealed the fact that most of the tests were done on conventional machines. She also created a culture of secrecy and intimidation within her company, silencing anyone who questioned or challenged her. After being found guilty on four counts of fraud, she is the most glaring example of good storytelling for a bad purpose.

"The most powerful person in the world is the storyteller. The storyteller sets the vision, values, and agenda of an entire generation that is to come."

STEVE JOBS

The unfortunate truth is that crafting a disingenuous or inauthentic origin story is not as rare as we'd hope. With PR and marketing departments converging, often referred to as activation teams, companies try to create authenticity that isn't there (to be explored later). Marketers have an essential role to play in every business, but you – the founder and CEO – need to own your company's story and lead by example. Collaborate with your marketing team, actively engage in shaping, embodying and living the story. All too often, smart communications and marketing people come up with clever advertising campaigns and internal communication strategies that align with the vision. Unless you, the CEO, and other senior managers are owning and driving those messages, your company's mandate, strategy, internal cohesion, and public-facing brand can fracture.

The push to share our stories with the marketing department instead of waiting for a script is a growing trend that demonstrates how seriously businesses are taking their narrative. Many companies now teach storytelling skills to their top executives. Procter and Gamble (P&G) approached Hollywood movie directors to train its top brass on how to lead through storytelling. All of the senior leadership team at Nike are also so-called 'corporate storytellers.' Even 3M has taken a bold step by replacing bullet points with 'strategic narratives.' Use stories to launch your business, build your mandate, motivate your team, expand your markets, and make a community from your customers. The sky will be your entrepreneurial limit. Alternatively, if you're like Richard Branson or Elon Musk, you won't stop there.

Branson, the eccentric head of the Virgin Group and space flight mogul places an enormous emphasis on storytelling within his businesses. He sometimes gathers his employees around a campfire to talk, believing the results are higher engagement, better ideas, and more collaboration.[8] In a 2017 article for Virgin.com, Branson wrote:

The best way to get somebody to take in something you want to share – a lesson, a business pitch, anything – is to do it in the form of a story. When we hear stories, we can be simultaneously involved in the tale. We can empathize, relate, and understand far more that way. The ability to tell a story with passion, humor, and heart will help build trust. When I am listening to business pitches, if I can understand the vision of the entrepreneur through their storytelling, I am far more likely to get interested. The purpose and products of the business still need to be right, but storytelling can help to bring these to life.[9]

The Good

Branson is a seasoned storyteller and has the business chops to make people sit up and take note. However, today, telling stories that resonate with people is getting harder, as the society is continuously evolving, it is more fragmented than ever, people are far more educated, and critical thinking has taught us how to *doubt everything*. If you've lived in New York (like me), you always have an extra eye out for a scam. Our world is full of unverified journalism, photoshop, paid advertorials, and filters of every kind. Each bending the truth in various ways. Sometimes we like a bit of escapism – a little stretching of reality – but if it's a lie painted as a fact, the audience will revolt more often than not.

Richard Branson is a good storyteller in the business world because he uses stories to spark new ideas. Branson believes that telling a story is one of the best ways to come up with innovative solutions and products. He likes to gather his team around a campfire to exchange stories and brainstorm. Branson knows that the Virgin story, with its highs and lows, attracts customers and employees who want to be part of it. He says, "We would be nothing without our story"[10]. He also uses it to inspire others. Branson shares his own stories of adventure, risk, and resilience to motivate people to pursue their dreams and overcome challenges. He says, "If your life is one long success story, it won't make for a good read"[11].

So how do we weave a good one? This comes back to the heart of every story: character, conflict, resolution.

On conflict, researcher Paul Zak has found that to really grab and hold an audience's attention, stories need to develop tension throughout the narrative: "If the story is able to create that tension then it is likely that attentive viewers/listeners will come to share the emotions of the characters in it, and after it ends, likely to continue mimicking the feelings and behaviors of those characters."[12]

That sharing of emotion is increased depending on the relatability of the characters involved. Sometimes that comes down to personal preference: are we partial to the knight on the white horse or the damsel in distress or the bad boy or the girl-next-door? When we begin to connect emotionally with a story and its characters, that's called "transportation."[13] Transportation stimulates our brains to identify with the character in the story. If they feel sad, we feel sad. If they're escaping from the bad guy, our palms might sweat as we will them to survive. If you're watching a free diver underwater, you might subconsciously hold your breath.

As long as the character in your story (who, in the case of your business, is likely you) is likable enough, people will be able to relate. Before you write your story, make sure you can truly embody the person you're envisioning.

As horrible as it sounds, there is no story more engaging than a car accident. Anyone who's ever driven by a car wreck knows it's impossible to disregard, no matter how hard you try to look away. What you know when you see an accident is real people are involved; this accident may have changed or even ended someone's life, or at the very least, ruined their day; and you want to hear that everybody survived and is going to be okay. Tension, struggle, conflict – these things sell newspapers. What do we all like after a potent dose of conflict? Resolution. The victim is going to be okay. The bad guy is going to jail. The hard worker is reaping his reward. Tell people your struggle, your problem, your barrier, and then invite them to come along with you as you find the resolution.

How about creating our own pitch using a character, conflict resolution approach?

Characters

James Breton: The charismatic and experienced Creative Director, well-known for thinking out of the box.
Joanna Brown: A talented copywriter eager to prove herself by bringing a fresh perspective.
Tyler Cole: The confident and resourceful Account Executive.
Edward: The client, representing a leading luxury car brand.

Conflict

In the high-pressure pitch room, tension fills the air as the team presents their campaign concept for the luxury car brand. James, Joanna, and Tyler have poured their creative energy into a daring and innovative concept that pushes the boundaries of traditional car advertisements. However, Edward, the client, with a poker face is skeptical. He has reservations about departing from the brand's tried-and-true image as he's used to safe, conventional campaigns, and this bold idea feels risky. The atmosphere is charged with uncertainty now.

As James passionately pitches the concept, he faces Edward's resistance and skepticism. The conflict lies in convincing the client that taking this creative leap will differentiate their brand, captivate a younger audience, and redefine luxury in the automotive industry. The risk is that Edward might reject the idea, and the team could lose a prestigious client.

Resolution

Joanna steps in, offering a compelling narrative that resonates with Edward's desire to remain at the forefront of the industry. She paints a vivid picture of how the campaign will make the luxury car brand an icon of innovation and sophistication. Tyler follows up by emphasizing the emotional connection the campaign will forge with consumers.

As Edward listens, he begins to see the potential. He recognizes the bravery in this unconventional approach and how it aligns with the changing consumer landscape. The resolution occurs as Edward nods in agreement, intrigued by the team's vision. He decides to take the risk and green lights the daring campaign, setting the stage for a new era of luxury car advertising.

In this scenario, the characters (James, Joanna and Tyler) face a conflict rooted in creative risk-taking versus conventional approaches in advertising. The resolution hinges on persuasive storytelling that convinces the client to embrace innovation and set their brand apart in a highly competitive market, ultimately securing the success of the campaign.

The Bad

It's not all sunshine and unicorn tears. Storytelling in business can have its weaknesses and pitfalls, and entrepreneurs need to be aware of these. Unrelatable characters, unbelievable conflicts, and unsatisfactory resolutions are all common storytelling failings. Unfortunately, they are traps that many entrepreneurs have fallen into before, and many more will fall into in the future. In recent years, several high-profile entrepreneurs have paid the price, both monetarily and with jail time. An example is Billy McFarland and Fyre festival. With boundless enthusiasm, Billy promoted the Fyre Festival as a luxury music festival like no other. Through aggressive marketing and influencer endorsements, he portrayed the festival as a once-in-a-lifetime experience set on a private island with A-list musical acts, gourmet dining, and high-end accommodations. When attendees arrived at the Fyre Festival in April 2017, they encountered a complete disaster. The promised luxury accommodations were inadequate, basic necessities were lacking, and the gourmet meals were replaced with meager rations. Headlining musical acts had pulled out, leaving festival-goers in dire conditions. Billy McFarland faced legal consequences, including charges of wire fraud and a six-year prison sentence. The false brand story of an extravagant music festival turned into a colossal failure, causing financial losses, lawsuits, and reputational damage for McFarland.

Bad stories are built upon lies. Unfortunately, storytelling is an art form that con men and con women excel at. Stereotypical salespeople, fraudsters, and confidence tricksters can typically spin a marvelous tale. Social media is the new hothouse for these porky-tellers – a place where snappy sound bites and glossy photos are rarely fact-checked or subjected to critical questioning. One such storyteller from Australia hit the international media in recent years after building a whole foods/health empire based on her cancer diagnosis. Spoiler alert: she didn't actually have cancer. Belle Gibson tricked her hundreds of thousands of followers into believing she had saved her own life by only eating clean. She had undoubtedly spun a compelling narrative full of media. The story was gripping, but its substance has nowhere to be found (much to the dismay of the sick people who shirked traditional medicine in favor of Gibson's brand of wellbeing).

Likewise, an Instagram account "Californiaboy" with over 1.5 million followers was exposed as a fake influencer in 2017. The account purported to belong to a wealthy and adventurous Californian who showcased a lavish lifestyle filled with luxury cars, exotic travel, and designer clothing. It was later revealed that the account was operated by a marketing agency to attract sponsorship deals and paid promotions from brands eager to collaborate. Further investigations revealed that the whole persona was entirely fabricated, and the account was subsequently taken down by Instagram. So what've we learned from these bad narratives? Say no to lies because authenticity matters!

The Champions

The effectiveness of a business story hinges on whether you have a genuine narrative to share. There are great examples of entrepreneurial tales, and some not so great. One of my business story champions is Hamdi Ulukaya, founder and CEO of yogurt producer Chobani. Ulukaya is as textbook as it gets. Born to a Kurdish sheep farmer in Turkey, he embarked on a remarkable journey from nomad shepherd to self-made man. After emigrating to the U.S. in the nineties, Ulukaya started a small feta-cheese business, and in 2005 he undertook a daring step by buying a soon-to-be decommissioned yogurt factory. This marked the birth of his company, Chobani, a name rooted in Turkish signifying "shepherd." Chobani now enjoys more than one billion sales per year and employs upwards of 2,000 staff.

Ulukaya prides himself on bringing humanity back to business leadership. He argues that spreadsheets are "lazy" and fail to tell a CEO about people or communities, instead choosing to listen to people and their stories. Ulukaya has given away 10% of shares in Chobani to his 2,000+ employees, sharing the company's success directly with those who contribute to it. He has also initiated a job training program in conjunction with the College of Southern Idaho to provide job opportunities to local communities and address labor shortage in the area. He strongly advocates for fair wages and, on average, pays factory workers double the minimum wage.

In 2015, Ulukaya established the Tent Foundation, a nonprofit that encourages businesses to fight inequality by hiring refugees, investing in refugee-owned companies, and creating products and tailoring services to meet refugees' needs. The best part is about thirty percent of Ulukaya's Chobani workforce are immigrants or refugees. In 2016, Ulukaya announced that Chobani would grant six weeks of fully paid parental leave to new parents. His current goal for the company is to: "Make universal wellness happen sooner," and involves reducing Chobani's carbon footprint by up to 840 metric tons per year, cutting overall energy consumption by 17%, and donating over 325,000 cups of yogurt to food banks and community pantries in 2018.

Ulukaya's story – that of an environmental warrior, champion of the working class, and all-around top-notch guy – is not just his personal story, but mirrors the narrative of Chobani. You may not see any of this messaging in his products - his yogurt may not have his face stamped on the side with references to his good deeds, but the story is there. It is the very *foundation* of Ulukaya's company which demonstrates that entrepreneurship is not limited to one's background, inspires aspiring entrepreneurs to innovate, pursue their dreams and make a successful business out of it. His focus on creating a corporate culture that values employees and earns their loyalty;

efforts in refugee causes set an example of ethical business practices and a reminder that businesses can also make a positive impact on society. This success story of an immigrant highlights the importance of diversity and inclusivity in the business world. Last but not least, his life embodies the American dream - a narrative where success is the ultimate outcome of hard work, innovation and dedication. Your story doesn't need to be plastered everywhere for it to exist, but it will most certainly be evident with time.

Armed with this overview of storytelling, keep an eye out in the real world for how businesses employ story. The poet and social activist Muriel Rukeyser once wrote that "the Universe is made of stories, not of atoms." The more you think about your business narrative, the more you'll realize how important it is to your success (including the definition of success itself).

---

1. Aswath Damodaran, *Narrative and Numbers: The Value of Stories in Business*, (New York, Columbia University Press, 2017), vii.
2. Brené Brown, "The power of vulnerability" filmed June 2010 in Houston, Texas, TED video, 18:54, Accessed: https://www.ted.com/talks/brene_brown_on_vulnerability?language=en#t-66590
3. https://www.buzzfeed.com/alliehayes/growing-up-in-florida
4. https://www.buzzfeed.com/elainawahl/ohio
5. https://www.buzzfeed.com/andreborges/signs-from-india-that-will-make-you-cringe-and-lol
6. http://www.bbc.co.uk/newsbeat/article/34756100/the-bear-which-inspired-winnie-the-pooh-is-actually-a-girl
7. César Aliva et al., "Reading cinnamon activates olfactory brain regions," *NeuroImage*, Vol.32, Iss.2, 2006.
8. Carmine Gallo, "Richard Branson explains why storytelling is your competitive advantage," *Forbes*, October 17, 2017, Accessed: https://www.forbes.com/sites/carminegallo/2017/10/17/richard-branson-explains-why-storytelling-is-your-competitive-advantage/#2299a868deed
9.
10. https://www.forbes.com/sites/carminegallo/2017/10/17/richard-branson-explains-why-storytelling-is-your-competitive-advantage/

11. https://www.forbes.com/sites/carminegallo/2017/10/17/richard-branson-explains-why-storytelling-is-your-competitive-advantage/

12. Paul Zak, "Why your brain loves good storytelling," *HBR*, October 28, 2014, Accessed: https://hbr.org/2014/10/why-your-brain-loves-good-storytelling

13. " Tom van Laer, Stephanie Feiereisen and Luca Visconti, "Storytelling in the Digital Era: A Meta-Analysis of Relevant Moderators of the Narrative Transportation Effect," *Journal of Business Research*, Vol.96, No.1, 2019, pp.135-146.

CHAPTER 3

C.R.O.W.

HOW IMPROV CAN
Improve Your Business

There are a thousand ways to craft a story, and sometimes that's what makes it incredibly difficult. Before you actually sit down to start writing, everything is so much fun! Ideas bounce off the wall. Hundreds of fantastic titles for your autobiography run around your brain. Who knew there were so many excellent puns with your name? You are so creative. Writing is freakin' sweet!

Then you sit down to put it on digital paper, and something happens. That something is actually nothing at all. Thirty minutes of staring at a blank page and four trips to the snack cabinet go by. Nothing. It's not long before you're cursing the idea of writing anything down. What's the point? You think. Writing is stupid. No one cares anyway! After a couple of texts to friends about how hard it is to write, you start to reconsider any preconceived notion that it would happen automatically.

When it comes to storytelling, there are theories and there are techniques. Famous storytellers throughout history have given the world their fair share of weird and wonderful writing techniques. Dan Brown, the author of *Da Vinci Code*, hangs upside down to clear his head of writer's block. *Alice in Wonderland's* Lewis Carrol wrote only using purple ink. German poet, philosopher, and playwright, Friedrich Schiller let apples rot in his desk, believing the smell to be motivating. Victor Hugo got rid of his clothes while writing the Hunchback of Notre Dame to avoid the temptation of going out when he needed to write. While writing my last book, I would do twenty-five squats every thirty minutes to keep my blood flowing (somewhere on the internet, there's a study that says being active sparks creativity). No doubt you have your own working style and writing quirks that are of no real interest to me. One thing most writers have in common is structure. This chapter is about recognizing that structure.

Books, movies, and TV shows tell one overall story consisting of many scenes. The snowflake method. Beat sheets. The three-act structure. Carl Jung's merging 'male' and 'female' elements, for something a little more ...exotic. Storytelling is, as mentioned in the last chapter, fundamentally straightforward: A *character* has a *conflict* who finds a *resolution*. Within this world are two other terms worth mentioning, especially when placed in context to another. They are narrative and plot. Narrative, to me, is mostly interchangeable with story but is certainly open to interpretation. People select what parts of the story go into a narrative, thereby creating their own version. We will tell stories that create a long-term personal narrative. Plot relates more to memory, as was illustrated in the last chapter at the grocery store, than anything else. If you've seen a comedy in the previous ten years, Seth Rogan's name should come as no surprise. He defines plot in context to story like this:

"Plot is the things that are happening, and the story is what it's actually about. The plot should be the thing that seems the most important at first, and the story should be in there but almost unrecognizable. Then as the movie goes on that ratio should completely reverse itself."[1]

The balancing act of plot and story breaks down into the aforementioned series of scenes. "I created a service that locates restaurants which cater to people with celiac disease." That's not a story. It's information. "My name is Sarah. I am a celiac living in Chicago, so I created a service here that makes it easier for people like me to find food that won't kill us." That's a story - at its most basic, informational (and consumeristic) level. This structure – *character* (me), *conflict* (can't easily find food that won't kill me), *resolution* (my business) – is the baseline for a simple scene. It starts with Sarah wanting food that won't kill her and ends when she eats... or dies. Woof. What is the structure of that scene that conveys all that information so efficiently? Where do you start expanding on these critical beats? The answer, thanks to the years of being a nerd and studying Shakespeare, is C.R.O.W.

CROW is a mnemonic device used in the world of improvisational theater to help participants craft their on-stage scene work with precision and intention. It stands for Character, Relationship, Objective, and Where. Improv teaches listening, awareness of situations and relationships, clear communication, and how to deliver an audience the information they need to keep their attention.

As comedian, actor, and writer Scott Adsit puts it: "the rules of Improvisation apply beautifully to life."[2]

When I lived in Seattle, I worked for the digital agency Banyan Branch (absorbed by Deloitte Digital) and spent weekends doing improv comedy at Unexpected Productions, the city's downtown theater. At least once a month, we would be hired to run "Improv in Business" workshops for leadership teams, often at one of the city's larger companies like Microsoft. You don't need to be the theatrical type to take something from the practices of theatrical folk. Learning to recognize every boardroom, lunch meeting, and networking event as a live scene will open the gates to effective communications everywhere. The same skills that make great theater and entertainment can also help grow your business. Like much of this journey, CROW begins with you.

Character

Character is the first and most important of CROW's four pillars relating to the context of this book. Character is the heart. It dictates your company's ethics, its mission , its positioning in the market, its communication, and consumer acquisition strategy. In some cases, it can even define the nature of products or services to offer.

The best stories lead us to projection, identification, empathy, imitation, and imagination. If your audience is identifying with you, feeling compassion for you, or wants to imitate you – then you've done something right with your story. To achieve that kind of emotional reaction, entrepreneurs need to make some decisions right off the bat. Sit down with a pen and paper and make notes about who you are, who you want to be, and how you'd like to be perceived. In improv, you need to make quick decisions about how you present yourself – how you move, speak, stand, and act. Flesh this out early, and you'll be building on a more solid foundation.

It's also important to consider how you see other people – those you encounter in your daily life. With any person we meet or see – be that in business, movies, or the real world – we react to them one of the following ways:

1. I want to be that person.
2. I don't want to be that person.
3. I am that person.

Let's take Bill Gates as an example – at one time, the richest man in the world. Personally, I want to be him because he's intelligent, passionate, caring, and purposeful. These are things I aspire to be in my own life. I want to be Bill Gates because he has managed to achieve so much without sacrificing his morality. I want to be him because he married someone who elevates and challenges him. He has children who are not on a reality TV show. He leads the way in giving back and influences others in high power positions to use their stature in similar ways.

On the other side of the coin, I *don't* want to be Bill Gates. I don't want to lose my privacy. I don't want to be stopped in the street by people who don't know me. I don't want to feel like people always want something from me.

Then, last of all, there's a sense of reflection. I *am* Bill Gates. I see parts of me in parts of him. I'm someone who seeks to make a positive change in the world. I like to read, challenge myself to learn new things, travel, and listen. I'm a bit of a nerd, although we all tend to think this of ourselves. I also don't know how to dress with much fashion sense but will happily wear what others put on me.

Ok now, let's try this again with my Armenian counterpart, Kim Kardashian. I do *NOT* want to be her. I don't want a public sex tape. I don't want a film crew to capture my entire life. I don't want pressure on my physical appearance. There are a lot of reasons a celebrity like her does not appeal to me. Then again, there's a big part of her that creates an undeniable connection. We share the bond of family heritage. We're both Armenian. Like religion, family background draws a direct line into our veins. Knowing that we eat the same food, hear the same stories, and share physical characteristics makes for absolute similarities.

Finally, who are we kidding? Of course I want to be her! She never has to worry about money. She has virtually unlimited access to the world. She is seen by many as beautiful and inspirational. Her family members are some of her closest friends. Plus, she was married to arguably the most influential producer/rapper of our time. Truth be told, I even tweeted at her once. She didn't tweet back, but I always wondered what if...

Do this exercise with a few characters you're familiar with – whether they be fictional, friends, or famous folk. It's essential to understand how you perceive others so that you better know how to represent yourself. You are not merely *you*. You are the version of yourself you choose to present to the world. To make that representation effectively, you need to learn how to excavate the many versions of you that you are. Remember the three ways we react to people or characters are not mutually exclusive . The people we become most invested in are people with whom we experience all three.

Let's talk about me for a second. I was a fat kid growing up. During fourth and fifth grade, the private elementary school I attended required all boys wear the same khaki pants. When my mother took me to the uniform store, they measured me with no regard for the scars they were about to create. "We don't have any regular sizes that fit him, but we're going to have him try on a waist size 32 *husky*." She said that. Husky. What's worse is it's actually the official term. Bigger around the waist without the height. Imagine?

Every night, I would sit my husky ass at the dinner table across from my brother and his lightning-fast metabolism. Night after night, I'd hope that I would get seconds, but my parents relegated anything extra to my older brother. It was, in hindsight, the healthy thing to do. I decided the way to get around this was to change my career trajectory. "I'm going to be the first American sumo-wrestler," I'd proclaim.

I figured eating professionally would be my workaround. Unfortunately, that didn't happen. I grew up and lost the pounds after my aunt "sponsored" a Weight Watchers program for me in 7th grade (seriously).

These experiences are still a part of who I am – a husky, food-loving, wannabe sumo-wrestler. Although this is a minor detail from my adolescence, it's as part of my story that I can access if it fits one of the narratives I'm pushing. Trust me; this will have a secure place in it if I ever build a business around body image or health. Recognizing and vocalizing these parts of my life leave touch points for customers, audiences, employees, and others to relate to me. The more touch points an audience has to relate or react to in a story, the better chances we have of it being a good one.

Let's try to delve deeper into the contrasting roles that characters play in storytelling vs. real-life business - offer valuable insights into the dynamics of character portrayal. In a story, movie or a novel the character (Sherlock Holmes or Wednesday Addams) play a crucial role in advancing the plot and conveying the themes to connect with the audience at an emotional level. Likewise, it is the responsibility of the CEO or a project manager to keep the business going towards success. Their diverse backgrounds, experiences and motivations contribute to the narrative's richness. One thing important to mention here is, just as in movies, there are many supporting characters besides the main character, similarly, in businesses, apart from the CEO, there are characters such as employees, investors, and executives, etc who play equally important roles. As far as the emotional connection with the customers is concerned it might not be on a similar level to stories. For example, people might appreciate the efficiency of a delivery person but not form the same emotional bond as they would with a fictional character. Remember! you can still get the most out of it.

On the other hand, characters in stories often face internal and external conflicts that drive the plot. The resolution of these conflicts contributes to the story's climax and conclusion. What happens in a business then? Characters in business scenarios encounter conflicts related to financial decisions, market competition, human relations, CRM, compliances, innovation and what not. These conflicts are typically resolved in a pragmatic manner to achieve business objectives. Lastly, creators utilize characters as conduits for artistic expression in storytelling. Characters like Atticus Finch in "To Kill a Mockingbird" and Elizabeth Bennet in "Pride and Prejudice" are not mere players but intricate personas crafted to explore themes, symbolism, and societal issues. Atticus embodies moral integrity and justice, enabling Harper Lee to tackle racial discrimination. Elizabeth, with her wit and independence, helps Jane Austen delve into themes of class and gender. These characters transcend fiction, symbolizing the broader themes authors wish to convey, enriching the storytelling experience. However in a business domain there is no artistic expression but rather characters are more practical, concerned for task execution, decision-making and time management. Their actions and decisions are guided by the pursuit of increased revenue, market share, efficiency, and profitability. Within this context, leadership often emphasizes the practical aspects of achieving business success. While effective leaders may indeed provide inspiration and a visionary direction, their primary objective revolves around the attainment of tangible business objectives and goals. In essence, while there may be elements of inspiration and vision in corporate leadership, the overarching aim remains the advancement of the organization's interests and the realization of its strategic objectives.

Consider CROW's first part as it relates to Ethan Brown, the founder and CEO of Beyond Meat™. Beyond Meat is a plant-based protein producer, making meat-like patties from soy. Brown's business story helps lend his company credibility, encourages relatability and empathy from consumers, and underpins his business mandate:

I grew up in the city, in Washington, DC, and College Park, Maryland. But my dad grew up in the country and bought a farm to start a weekend dairy operation with less than 100 Holstein cows. I fell in love with life outdoors and the animals that surrounded us. I began to question the difference between animals in the agricultural system and the ones we kept as pets. And as I became an adult, I understood that it was a cultural, and not biological, justification for the difference.[3]

In establishing a public-facing character, Brown recognizes the importance of his emotive nature of business. He has skillfully put together his personal narrative, knowing that it resonates deeply with people who share love for the outdoors and animals. Through references to his childhood, he not only makes his story relatable but also paints a picture of himself as a regular, intelligent, rural guy with a strength of conviction. This character portrayal forms a compelling foundation for his role as the driving force behind Beyond Meat.

Relationship

Relationships are power. Whether we have the lens of entertainment or business, the power dynamic of a relationship dictates the tone of the scene. There are three types of relationships we will examine: neutral, authority, and shifting. Neutral relationships generally include friends, cousins, and coworkers. These relationships exist where neither party holds any clear or necessary advantage over the other. Boss-worker, prisoner-warden, owner-pet, and teacher-student exemplify authority relationships. These submissive-dominant relationships give one person the upper hand over another. Finally, there are shifting relationships, where there's a transfer of power over time. Think about a parent-child or couples. The most engaging relationships are ones where the power dynamic shifts over time. The student becomes the teacher. The intern becomes the boss. The girlfriend goes from in love to disinterested. We have different relationships with different people, places, and things that predicate how we show up even without noticing.

In business, we are often told that relationships are everything. It makes sense then that in business storytelling relationships are given special attention. How do the people in the room change how you talk, walk, and act? Even before you have an objective, relationships are what drive your behavior as an entrepreneur. The relationship of an entrepreneur with their mentor is worth mentioning. It is not just about being motivated by someone but grooms entrepreneurs into more capable, knowledgeable, and resilient individuals. It provides a valuable support system throughout their entrepreneurial journey and accelerates their personal and professional growth. The mentor's guidance and wisdom are instrumental in shaping the entrepreneur's success. For instance, an entrepreneur (of any level) who deeply admires the vision and innovation of Elon Musk may be motivated to pursue audacious goals in space exploration or EVs. Such mentors instill a sense of purpose and ambition by igniting one's entrepreneurial spirit. Similarly, positive reinforcement in other words, a little support (celebrating a small milestone) from friends, family, industry peers, investors, even employees and customers has a profound influence on mental health and personal/professional behavior of an entrepreneur. It boosts his confidence and helps strengthen relationships.

How networks and communities influence an entrepreneur? Being a part of these interconnected ecosystems offers a wealth of resources, support, and opportunities that can significantly influence an entrepreneur's path. They serve as knowledge-sharing platforms where entrepreneurs can gain insights, industry-specific expertise, and best practices from their peers. This collective wisdom informs their decisions and strategies, potentially saving them from costly mistakes. Besides, relationships with such networks offer emotional support as well, serving as a refuge during challenging times and fostering a sense of camaraderie.

Your relationships go beyond personal. We all have relationships with money, fame, and the problem we intend to solve. Before stepping foot towards a marketing plan, you need to ask yourself: how are my relationships affecting my behavior? I guarantee that in a room of entrepreneurs with clothing lines for cancer patients, the ones who have had cancer will act differently. Identify the relationships to the people, places, and things in your "scene" and walk away with a better sense of your product, the customer (current and potential), and self.

You are the heart of your company, but other people are the lungs. They are your customers, your coworkers, your staff, your supporters, your critics, your networks, media, suppliers, competitors, and even their third-grade teacher who told you you'd never amount to anything. Stories need to establish relationships in order to touch on their human core and give real meaning to your business.

These relationships influence all aspects of your journey, and they will undoubtedly be a part of your story. They are part of your internal memos and communications to your employees. They are part of your daily operations and dealings with suppliers. You don't just need to recognize and understand those relationships in your mind. You also need to be able to communicate about them and to them.

Storytelling isn't a one-dimensional playing field – you are not merely an orator with a captive audience. You need to consider relationships in terms of external storytelling, yes, but don't forget to tell stories *to* people, not just about people. Each relationship in your business is going to be unique, and you won't treat the bank manager the same way you treat your suppliers. CROW is about relationships, but use it *in* your relationships too. Learn what is unique about the relationship you're walking into. Learn what that person likes, what makes them tick, and approach your interactions accordingly.

In the story of Ethan Brown's Beyond Meat, he makes a point of explaining his relationship to consumers. Brown knows that plant-based meats are controversial and looked down on by many meat-eaters. He understands his market and, by explaining the connection he sees between his product and the meat-eating consumer, can reassure that customer segment of his intentions:

We have to prove that we can do this because the only thing that I know with absolute certainty about the consumer is that the consumer loves meat. You know most of us do. Around 94 percent of the population here in the United States. And so that's a really clear target for me. If I start to try to create a new flavor profile with a new consistency, that's really hard. And what I want to do is prove through science that you don't need the animal to produce a piece of meat and then I have a ton of freedom after that, but I feel like we need to pass through that or else we just become one of many other choices.[4]

Objective

The main objective of running a business is, at face value, simple. However, few people start a business with only one objective in mind: maximizing profits. Each of those objectives carries different weight, and those stakes (not Ethan Brown's kind) will determine the urgency for which we approach them. How, then, are they part of our business story, and how does their shifting urgency affect your story?

The objective and stakes of your business are distinct but closely intertwined. Are we doing this to make money? To meet market demand? Make a name for ourselves? Save the planet? Give back to the community? All of the above? And what happens if we don't accomplish our objective? Do we lose money? Does a competitor 'win'? Do we lose professional relevance? Does the human race have that much less time on earth?

Every character needs motivation. Your motivation builds on your choice to offer the product or service you offer. It helps set your principles, your growth goals, your relationships with investors, consumers, and staff. In improv, motivations are broken down into two categories: micro and macro.

A micro objective would be something like: turn on the room light.

A macro objective could be: find my pants.

Micro objectives are accomplished to complete the macro objective. I can't find my pants until I turn the light on. Ethan Brown has four critical objectives for Beyond Meat, what he calls the "four horsemen." Those are:

- To produce a low-cost alternative to meat
- A way to save the environment
- A way to be healthier
- A way to improve animal welfare.[5]

Brown demonstrates the way he distinguishes between micro and macro objectives in this interview:

We refer to those as the four horsemen, and they're the pillars of why we're doing what we're doing, but we don't tend to market around each one of them. In fact, the campaign that we have this year for our marketing platform is called the "Center of the Plate" campaign, and there are three pieces to it. The first is to prove the taste and texture of our products, which includes sampling, appearing on TV shows and radio, and having people sample it live and attest to the quality of it. The second is to demystify plant protein. There's a lot of misconceptions around plant proteins, and whether it's processed, and if it's a genuinely healthy thing to be giving my kids, and so we're putting together a farm-to-table video that describes the simple process that's at play when you create meat directly from plants, and really it's a heating, cooling, and pressure process that we use, so it's an effort to make moms particularly comfortable about feeding this to their families. The third piece is to attack the misconceptions about plant protein. For that piece, we hired the architect for the "Got Milk" campaign, and said that we'd like them to make the same type of messaging around plant protein. ... this is an effort to say that this is an evolution in meat. This is better, more nutrient-dense that meat, and athletes particularly are endorsing it because it's a very clean fuel. So we're building a campaign around that to 1) get people to taste the product, 2) to have them comfortable with our process, and 3) to get them to realize that this is, in fact, the cleanest fuel for their body.[6]

Don't forget, though, that it's not all about you. To tell your story and meet your objectives, you also need to consider the objectives of buyers. Customers want education, and they want to buy from a place of trust. Understand the goals of your consumers, and you can refine your own micro objectives to suit. It may be that your audience is not interested in products alone – that they're looking to engage with you, your story, a cause. Your micro objectives, therefore, need to play to those ends. To build trust, to create a brand, to gather a community. Only then can you start converting that community into sales – your macro objective. As Cheryl Platz, a UX Design Lead at quoted while at Microsoft contends:

It is when we lose sight of customer objectives that we risk failing our customers. Autoplay videos on social media sites are relatively controversial and widely derided. Why? In part, because a common customer objective when visiting a social media site is "discreetly take a break or pass the time in environments not conducive to sound." Or in other words, a common objective is "Stay connected to people I care about during my workday without getting in trouble." In other cases, autoplay videos fail because a different customer persona seeks to minimize their data plan usage.[7]

Where

We act and react differently based on our environment. We're creatures of place and children of circumstance. We have intrinsic characteristics, but much of our surroundings have an undeniable influence on our decision-making. Have you ever loaded up to tell a joke at someone else's expense, and looked to see if they were around? Place has a more significant bearing on your business story than you imagine. The environment (both place and circumstantial) dictates, among other things:

- Market Sophistication
- Competitive Landscape
- Social Trends
- Economic Status

In the less sophisticated markets (consumers with limited knowledge of the product/service), the businesses can pull off some moves by positioning themselves as pioneers and crafting simple educational brand stories, focused on problem solving and basic needs. The decisions are influenced by accessibility and ease of wallet, building trust and long-term relationships with the customers. On the contrary, in highly sophisticated markets, things get a bit complex and well-informed decision-making is needed. Take Xiaomi, for example, in China and Pakistan, they have gained prominence by offering high-quality smartphones at competitive prices as they are still a growing market for smartphones. However, in the likes of the United States, brands like Apple and Samsung emphasize advanced features, design, and ecosystem integration in their brand stories because they cater to tech-savvy consumers who expect cutting-edge innovation.

For any business, the market competition is like a dance partner. You're always watching their moves and adjusting your steps. No doubt, the competitive landscape of the business world is highly dynamic, the market conditions change in no time. New entrants, shifting consumer preferences, brand images and technological advancements all can disrupt your well-crafted decisions. And in the end, sometimes, a small shift in the business landscape can make you throw your whole game plan out the window. It's like having to change your entire playbook because the field's changed, and you've got to roll with it. Before COVID-19 many restaurants heavily relied on dine-in customers, offering sit-down dining experiences as their primary revenue source. During COVID-19 with lockdowns and restrictions in place, dine-in services became nearly impossible. Entrepreneurs in the restaurant industry had to pivot quickly. They embraced takeout and delivery services, implemented strict safety measures, and adjusted their menus to cater to the changing consumer preferences for at-home dining. Even after the COVID-19 when restrictions eased, the shift toward takeout and delivery services remained a significant part of their business models. Many restaurants invested in online ordering platforms, contactless payment systems, and enhanced delivery infrastructure to meet evolving customer expectations.

In the ever-evolving landscape of entrepreneurship, staying

in sync with social trends is like having a SUPERPOWER. Sometimes, it's like the wind in the sails, propelling businesses in exciting directions. For instance, the growing emphasis on sustainability and environmental responsibility has led many businesses to reevaluate their decisions. Companies like Patagonia have not only integrated eco-friendly materials into their products but have also engaged in environmental activism, aligning with the trend toward ethical consumerism. Similarly, the rise of remote work and flexible schedules, harnessed the trend of gig work. Big names are hiring freelancers across the globe to avoid additional costs of additional hiring, bringing specialized skills on the table, reduced administrative burden and quick turnaround. Was it like this before? Certainly not!

Consider the coffee industry's giants, Starbucks and Dunkin' (now Dunkin' Brands Group, Inc.). Starbucks positioned itself as a premium coffee brand, targeting consumers willing to pay a premium for artisanal coffee experiences. In contrast, Dunkin' catered to cost-conscious customers, offering more affordable coffee and quick-service options. These divergent strategies were rooted in understanding and aligning with the economic status of their target markets. Starbucks thrived in upscale urban areas, while Dunkin' excelled in more price-sensitive regions. Such decisions reflect how businesses strategically adapt to economic realities to capture market segments and stay profitable.

Our sensitivities and perceptions are different depending on place and circumstance. Our senses can be lit up by our surroundings. The environment your story is set in helps to support the story you're telling about the main character (you), your relationships, and your business objective.

. . .

The 'where' in CROW is often the poor cousin to the other three building blocks, but don't neglect it. As Cheryl Platz puts it, "Contextual inquiry is an excellent research tool to help us define and understand the where, and it's often a lost art. We don't know what we don't know about a customer environment until we see it ourselves."[8]

In the Beyond Meat business, founder Ethan Brown has been extremely conscious of the environment he is operating within and plays it to the company's advantage. In such a new, innovative sphere, he has developed an astute understanding of the global environment in which he is operating, taking into account that:

- Attitudes toward meat are changing
- Animal welfare is of increasing concern to consumers
- Health concerns are driving more and more people toward plant-based diets

Brown is also well-versed at operating within diverse environments and telling the story of those environments. In his media appearances he reveals the various facets of his business story by appearing:

- In the lab (demonstrating his knowledge and the scientific credibility of his business)
- At the stock exchange (having listed Beyond Meat in 2019, Brown is inviting investors to back the plant-based meat movement – and they are, with Beyond Meat enjoying the best performing US IPO in nearly two decades)

- In fast-food outfits (Brown has introduced the 'Beyond Burger' patty to Carl's Jr – bringing meat-free meat options to the fast-food market)

Storytelling in business is about the thousands of scenes you are actively creating and participating in. Documenting your story 'plan' using CROW does not mean that your character, your personality, your*self* need fixing. Far from it. You will need a baseline, but aside from that – you must be malleable. In each business interaction, you need to run the CROW scenario in your head. Who am I dealing with? Which version of myself do I need to play to get the best outcome? Do I need to play an educational role, or a managerial one – do I need to be submissive on this occasion, or demonstrate my leadership? Then ask what's happening in your various business relationships. Are they healthy? Do you need to pay closer attention to some over others this quarter? What are your objectives – micro and macro? Do you need adjusting based on your relationships, or the environment you're working in? And the environment itself. Are you trying to sell snow plows in San Francisco? Surfboards in Sioux Falls? Awareness without acquiescence.

Now that you know how a good story is built and what makes a good story, it's time to go to the source material to uncover it. It should be no surprise by now that the source is you.

1. https://www.youtube.com/watch?v=DTmtFBPfRp4
2. Scott Adsit, quoted in "Stars stand up for Hollywood Arts," *Huffpost.com*, October 14, 2010, Accessed: https://www.huffpost.com/entry/stars-stand-up-for-hollyw_b_763527

3. Ethan Brown, quoted in Alice Park, "Why we don't need animals to keep enjoying meat," *Time.com*, June 6, 2019, Accessed: https://time.com/5601980/beyond-meat-ceo-ethan-brown-interview/

4. Ethan Brown, quoted in Zachary Mack, "Beyond Meat CEO Ethan Brown on how meatless burgers can still improve," *theverge.com*, June 13, 2019, Accessed: https://www.theverge.com/2019/6/13/18677921/beyond-meat-ceo-ethan-brown-meatless-burgers-gmos-sustainability

5. Ethan Brown, "Interview with Ethan Brown," *AnimalCharityEvalutors.com*, April 2015, Accessed: https://animalcharityevaluators.org/advocacy-interventions/advocacy-advice/learn-from-professionals/interview-with-ethan-brown-ceo-beyond-meat/

6. Ibid.

7. Cheryl Platz, "Catching CROW: Storytelling for UX Design," *Medium.com*, April 5, 2017, Accessed: https://medium.com/microsoft-design/catching-crow-storytelling-for-ux-design-5e5a0b6def99

8. Ibid.

CHAPTER 4

THE FOUR BIGGEST
QUESTIONS OF YOUR LIFE

"BECOMING *who we are is an ongoing process, and thank God
– because where's the fun in waking up one day and deciding
there's nowhere left to go?"* [1]

MICHELLE OBAMA

This is the advice Michelle Obama gives her daughters in
the August 2019 edition of *British Vogue*. It resonates in a world
that favors perfection, victory, labels, and quick judgments
overgrowth, learning, depth, and complexity. We shouldn't feel
compelled to define ourselves using titles and tick boxes, but we
also can't shy away from self-reflection and identity-mapping. In
an age where identity and business are so closely intertwined,
entrepreneurs must know themselves. And who knows you
better than you? Probably no one, but that doesn't mean you
have a good grip on it either. The introductions people give each
other are, by no coincidence, a good place to start.

How would you introduce somebody you've known for a
year? We're socially conditioned to define people in a relatively

prescribed way. Job. Age. Location. Place of birth. Marital status. Someone who has known me for a few months might deliver an intro as such:

> This is Ross. He's writing a book right now, and we met back when he used to work at Red Bull.

So that's me. Right? That's one person's perception of me – a person who has known me in a specific business/acquaintance setting, for a relatively short period. There's little room for someone to relate or react to me (remember the definition of a good story) before engaging in whatever mundane conversation will likely follow. What if somebody else introduced me? This someone has known me five years and loves to champion whatever adventure I'm on:

> This is Ross. He's writing a book right now and used to work as a video producer at Red Bull. We actually met, and this always sounds ridiculous, scooping poop at an organization for people with disabilities in Southeast Asia. He's one of the weirdest guys I know, and someone I consider one of my best friends. Did I mention he used to be the mascot for the Florida Gators?

You start to get a better sense of who I am, and you probably have a couple of questions. More importantly, there is more to relate or react to. In those four sentences, someone could build a genuine conversation about Florida, books, traveling, volunteering, sports, energy drinks, college, or video production.

Entrepreneurs are naturally hesitant to do this kind of "invisible work," and I completely understand. Remember this: The business is what you do. The story is why you do it. You are your business, or you are at least a representative of it. School teaches you to write a business or marketing plan. Unfortunately, it does not always teach you the uniqueness and personality required for long-term success. We're going to skip the line a bit and boil your complex psychology in the following pages. If it's not already clear, the four questions in this chapter fire me up. They are empowering. They provide a clear understanding of why you do what you do. Before we dive in, keep this logic in mind:

- Starting a business demands that you know where you're going.
- Knowing where you're going requires a plan for the future.
- The success of your plan will be influenced by how well you can tell your story.
- To tell your story, you need to know who you are.
- To know who you are, you must understand where you've come from.

This is the groundwork for your business. Skip it, and your foundations will buckle. Why you have chosen this particular business path has a direct tie to the four biggest questions of your life that everyone involved in your entrepreneurial journey will want to know: Who are you? How did you become that person? Who do you want to be? How are you going to become that person? If you think your business motivator is "to make money," well– think again.

⊏⊐

So here we go. Buckle up.
Let's find your story.

Who am I?

My name is Ross. I'm writing a book right now, and I used to work at Red Bull.

A simple answer to a complex question doesn't serve you. One that serves you takes time to understand. Still, it's one of the most rewarding and most necessary questions that young entrepreneurs can ask themselves. A question that delves them into self-identity, values, aspirations and purpose, finding the answer can prove crucial in shaping their entrepreneurial path. However, there's no single answer, but your actions should back it. Take a moment and think about who you are with, as defined by you.

- What are my daily habits?
- How do I spend my spare time?
- What are my guilty pleasures?
- Where do I donate money?
- What kind of food do I eat?
- Who are my five closest friends?
- How do I define my style?
- What are my finances?
- What are my family relationships?
- How do I define happiness?
- When am I the happiest?
- What am I thankful for?
- What is missing?
- Where do I call home?
- What do I have better than most?
- What political issues do I feel most informed about?

In the words of legendary rapper Rakim: "I'm the R to A to

the K-I-M, if I wasn't, then why would I say I am?"[2] As an entrepreneur, you will have a degree of control over the business trajectory, its decisions, strategies, and, ultimately, the outcomes. When it comes to defining who you are, however, you retain total control. Personal identity is a distinct aspect of life for every entrepreneur which may include values, beliefs, character and presentation in front of the world. Your friends, family, colleagues, press, social audience, and sometimes even strangers will corroborate this image or challenge it. Ultimately, you know what is right. You are bound in the memory of others by limited interactions that will hopefully represent your truth. Of course, we are not immune to a bad day, a nasty tweet, or incongruent behavior. Storytime...

Growing up in Orlando, I was no stranger to golf. I would sell golf balls I'd found around the local course. My parents, knowing about my business, took me to the Arnold Palmer Invitational about an hour away from where we lived. We waited there for one reason: see Tiger Woods. The game's megastar had fans stacked by the white guard fences to get an autograph. We waited and waited and then, just like that, we saw him in his signature red shirt, black pants, and black hat. When Tiger finished the hole, I stuck my little arm out for an autograph.

"Tiger, over here!" I yelped in an adolescent voice that would challenge any chipmunk effect. My plea, against the others, might as well have not existed.

"He's not doing pictures or autographs. Thank you," his handler sharply fired out. Tiger walked by without a look. The crowd wasn't pleased. Shortly after, I remember listening to everyone's murmur. The consensus was that he's an asshole because everyone's been waiting all day. The next time Tiger's name was mentioned in conversation, I chimed in.

"I saw him once. He was an asshole," I'd describe. That's who he was to me. An asshole. It was not until later that I came to understand, one interaction does not define a person.

Given that he was later outed as a serial adulterer and drunk driver, I could surely connect the dots, but that's a bit much to see my interaction as prophetic. I look back and think how ridiculous it was for me to gossip or judge an interaction that virtually didn't exist. Yet, we do it all the time.

Being an entrepreneur (and so a public figure) puts you in the spotlight as a leader. As a leader, the definition of your character will be put into question and continuously be tested by others. In the words of Eminem, who rebirthed a line from the aforementioned rapper Rakim: "I am whatever you say I am, if I wasn't then why would I say I am?"

"Who am I?" is not only who you think you are, but also how others see you. Identify why you are where you are, and you will be a step closer to having your "this is me" elevator pitch.

Let me start by saying, a personality test does not tell you who you are. Neither does a horoscope, a cartoon quiz, or a movie poll. Many of us have taken the Myers-Briggs personality test, usually in a professional setting, and been classified as either introverted or extroverted, thinking or feeling, judging or perceiving. This type of analysis is certainly useful at prompting discussions about how we work, and the different personalities we work with, but sometimes the result can be limiting. They leave us with the notion that personality is a rigid thing – that we "are who we are" and cannot possibly exhibit traits from outside that mold.

There's a lot to be said for appreciating the nuance of perception. Remember a few years back, when the "What I actually do" meme was doing the rounds on social media? It gave different perspectives on one career. The pictures illustrate what society thinks I do, what my Mom thinks I do, what I actually do, and so on. In the same vein, and borrowing from the flawless psychology of internet meme architects, ask yourself:

- How does society see me?
- How does my family see me?
- How do my friends describe me?
- What would my colleagues say about my work ethic?
- What does Google have to say about me?
- And, most importantly, how do I feel about these perspectives?

Who I am depends a lot more on relationships than on achievements. They hold the key to the perspectives that make who I am:

- Ross is a wonderful son. [Dad]
- Ross brings unique energy into every room. [Boss]
- Ross is more like a family member than a founder. [Investor]
- Ross has a great arm. [Dog]

In each of the above introductions, I am, of course, the same person. Depending on relationships and circumstances, a different version of me becomes more apparent. We're all different things to different people – sometimes thanks to the changeable way we present ourselves to others, and sometimes due to their unique reading of us. If I were to sit down and read others' descriptions of my character, no doubt many of the critical themes would give me pause for thought. Both because of the apparent consensus around some of my strongest traits, but also the choice of some characteristics over others.

Then, consider the following:

- Does any group see me in a completely inauthentic way? If so, how am I representing myself that led them to that conclusion?
- Does anybody see me in a way that has truth to it, but doesn't sit well with me? If so, what can I change about myself to address that inconvenient truth?
- Which perceptions of myself do I most wish to embody?
- Why do some of these differ so much from my version of myself?

Sometimes external perceptions can differ wildly from the truth. We've all met that introverted person who turns out to be an exotic dancer (mostly if you've been to Portland), or the angry, macho dude who secretly has a passion for My Little Pony (see: Bronies). Sometimes that's because we're giving an inauthentic impression, either through fear, or a misguided desire to impress, toe-the-line, or stand out. Sometimes it's because we don't want to give all of ourselves away to the world, and that's *okay*. You don't have to give all of yourself to everyone else — some cards you may like to keep close to your chest.

The tightrope to walk is this: if you're an entrepreneur wanting to build a business presence and sincerity is essential to your brand, then withholding critical parts of who you are may hinder growth. To that end, you'll need to dig a little deeper – to take a quick look into the rearview mirror. When I graduated high school, my friend Matt's Mom reminded me, "To know where you're going, you have to know where you came from."

How Did I Become That Person?

We are products of so many different factors and influences, and we aren't here to analyze every event in your camera roll. That doesn't mean probing your past is purely a therapist's job, nor that it should be filed away in the "too hard" basket. If you're going through the motions of identifying who you are, then you owe it to yourself to complete the circuit with the even more challenging question: How did I become that person?

There is more hard evidence to this question than any other question. Years of information filed away in our memory awaits to be accessed. Think about school, awards, losses, loves, injuries, the spelling bee competition you got second place in (I will never misspell raspberry ever again), and all the little interactions with people you haven't thought of in years. Think about the seven steps that led you up to this moment in time. How did I get to the point of writing this book?

I am writing this book because I gave a lecture at UPenn. The teacher, Tina Wells, put the idea in my head to turn it into a book. I knew Tina from a fellowship trip I was invited on with 45 others working in the impact space. I qualified for this trip because of the impact work I'd done with the National Multiple Sclerosis Society for the past eight years when my older brother was diagnosed with MS. I would've never even thought of writing a second book if I hadn't written the first one. I would've never written the first one if Ingrid B. didn't donate to my Kickstarter campaign in the last hour. And so on, and so on. Magical discoveries can be found once we start understanding the trail that led us where we are right now. We do this in love stories, and now we're doing it with you.

There are over twenty theories of personality development – some are competing; others are different sides of the same coin. One of the most polarizing debates is the nature vs. nurture dichotomy, which often rears its head in ugly places with folks comparing the way others live. The contest is legitimate, but, in reality, the answer is that both nature and nurture play a part. The way we manifest in the world is far more complicated than one influence or another. We're complex beings, our personalities made up of our early childhood education, our later social learning, genetics, epigenetics, and choice.

Some things are often inherited. Simon Moore, a leader in psychology at London Metropolitan University, says "sociability, for example, is probably more associated with your father than your mother, whilst educational-based intelligence is more related to mothers."[3] Other traits are products of the environment. Most importantly, it's important to note that for 95 percent of the population, characteristics are adaptable. Some people fall into extremes, but for most of us, our personalities can be highly changeable – most noticeably as we age, but even from week to week.

How can we best reflect on the remixed building blocks of our existence? Try looking at your life in its natural sections. You have a personal journey filled with family life and social life, and a professional journey filled with mentors and jobs and awards and losses. There are so many factors that sculpt us as individuals. Trace back to what makes you who you are by asking "why" about some of the following:

- Your temper
- An award you've won
- Feeling like an outcast
- An instrument or sport you play

- Whether or not you were picked for sports teams as a child
- Your opinion on pickles
- Your current favorite album
- If you prefer Twizzlers or Red Vines

The list is limitless. Identify who you are and how you came to be shaped in that way. Not only will you be able to communicate yourself and your business better to others, but you'll also be armed with the knowledge to help shape your future self. There are so many factors that sculpt us as individuals. We are shaped by triumph and loss and greed and generosity and tragedy and joy. How can you draw out the most pivotal influences in your life?

What about entrepreneurs? What are their traits? What makes their personality so special? A dash of risk-taking spirit, a generous sprinkle of innovation, a dollop of resilience, and a healthy serving of proactivity. These traits aren't handed out at birth; but are developed through life's experiences, like adding ingredients one by one to a recipe. That means, you can develop them too. Jack Ma, the visionary founder of Alibaba is an excellent example of entrepreneurial traits in action. He is well-known for his innovative spirit and ability to spot potential opportunities in a digital landscape. From co-founding Alibaba Group in 1999, at a time when e-commerce and internet-based businesses were relatively new concepts in China to turning it into a multifaceted technology conglomerate that includes e-commerce platforms (such as Alibaba.com and Taobao), cloud computing (Alibaba Cloud), digital payments (Alipay), and more shows his attitude towards risk-taking. Like other entrepreneurs, Ma has also faced several setbacks including rejections from investors, failed first venture (a translation service called China pages) and IPO suspension over his entrepreneurial journey.

However, despite these challenges, his resilience, proactivity and determination has proved that he is a real entrepreneur.

Something tells me you're not about to pull out a notebook and write down your key character traits – you'll probably hire a coach later for far more dollars than this book to force you into such exercises. Instead, think of a mentor or influential person in your life and remember which of their traits you have and how you came to think or act like that. Maybe you have no mentors, friends, family, pets, and you exist in a vacuum. In that case, we can pretend you are the subject of an upcoming movie.

Pixar pioneered a visual medium of storytelling, but they also formulated a way to connect with audiences. A few years back, former Pixar storyboard artist Emma Coats shared her learnings from working at the studio on Twitter and Tumblr in a list of 22 story basics.[4] Coats summarized the story structure like so:

> Once upon a time, there was ___.
> Every day, ___.
> One day ___.
> Because of that, ___.
> Because of *that*, ___.
> Until finally, ___.

If you take your self-directed therapy session and craft it into something digestible via the magic of a Pixar story, then you'll be staring at something that's starting to resemble a real-life, throw-it-on-your-'About Me'-page, "I'd like to thank the Academy" business story. Matt's Mom was right when she told me the importance of looking back, but there's a certain point where you have to put the past behind you.

Who Do I Want To Be?

"If you keep lookin' back, you gon' trip going forward."[5]

GUCCI MANE

Many of us spend a lot of time worrying about what we want to do with our lives, but much less time considering the person we'd like to be along the way. Don't confuse this question with "who do I want to be five years from now?" or "what do I want to be doing five years from now?" – That is the wrong direction for this conversation. In my experience, saying I'll be somewhere in five years almost guarantees that's the one thing I won't be (see: American Sumo wrestler). Life is dynamic and exciting, and even if you don't feel like a particularly impressive person, I'd still bet your future predictions will be off. Anyone who says they know what the future holds for themselves is lying. When you think about who you want to be, you are also thinking about how you want to be known and how you want to be remembered.

Processing your past and present may lead to excusing your future. Don't go down that path. You are an entrepreneur because you have something to say, something to fix, and a mission to accomplish. Clarify why you are doing, what you are doing in the context of who you want to be. A combination of logic, reality, and dreams set the possibilities. Limitations will humble and strengthen you along the way, but as you will develop with your business. If you haven't taken the time to consider *how* you'd like to grow, and who you'd be comfortable becoming, then you could find yourself having achieved an elite status without any sense of pure bliss.

I struggle with this question. It's incredibly open-ended and sets a lot of traps for disappointment or embarrassment. Once I answer it, I consider how silly it is. How is it that I am my own worst enemy? Writing a book is a bold task. I want to be someone who helps others connect with people through their personal stories and make life a little less lonely. That sounds cheesy as hell, but it's true.

Think about the people who made you who you are today. What do you admire about them? With that in mind, turn it back to yourself. What would you like your accomplishments to be? What is your moral imperative? How would you like to be remembered? If you could have something named after you, what would it be? A library? A hospital? A playground? A baby? A dog? A law? A disease? Consider these things and look back at what you wrote in the "until finally" section of your Pixar piece. Now rethink this exercise looking ahead. For me, one permutation looks like this:

- Once upon a time, there was an underemployed guy named Ross.
- Every day, he thought about writing a book about everything he'd learned making films.
- One day, he wrote a book about storytelling!
- Because of that, his friend hired him as a communications consultant.
- Because of that, he got hired by other companies to connect their business to their purpose.
- Until finally, Ross gave a TED Talk about the importance of bringing who we are into what we do.

This describes somebody who I want to be. It is a blueprint for a future self. Although your desired character is likely to change over time, try and hold on to some of the most active themes. Plug those into your moral compass, and let it have a significant impact on your future life. Being an entrepreneur is stressful. Being an entrepreneur with a larger company is sometimes even more stressful. Keep sight of who you want to be through the ups and downs. Whether you realize it or not, you're already becoming that person.

⊏━━⊐

How Do I Become That Person?

Welcome to your life. "Becoming that person" is the most exciting thing you will ever do. It is the journey, the endless obstacle, the story of *you*. As George Bernard Shaw once wrote, "Life is not about finding yourself. Life is about creating yourself."

But ... *how?* How do you take this envisioned person on paper and turn it into your reality? Once again, there is no exact formula. This is not a business plan. What works for someone, even someone similar to you, may have a tragically different effect. Role models, mentors, and heroes know where their choices have taken them. You do not (at least, not yet). The answer to this question will one day be to write your biography. There are thousands of books on how to be a better leader, manager, entrepreneur, lover, hater, investor, thief. Try the ones that speak to you. These books will throw ideas and methods worth testing. Quest for information that you need and discuss them where others are busy with the endless entertainment news cycle.

Answering this final question has a literal route and a somewhat cinematic path. The fairytale version of my story with a TED Talk ending has a literal path to achievement. Your literal path requires tangible work. This path will fill the pages of your pitch deck and your resume. You need to master skills, take classes, gain recognition, and more. You are climbing Mount

Everest, and climbing requires good health. Honestly, the trials (and success rate) of entrepreneurship make climbing Everest look like child's play.

Your thoughts, emotions, chemical balance, and behavior write your cinematic path. Are you the underdog? Did you inherit a business? What expectations exist? Who put them there? Business leaders, now more than ever, are susceptible to getting dragged through the mud. As you sail through the person you are and the person you want to become, new habits will battle the less favorable habits of old. This exercise wears us down. Charles Duhigg, in The Power of Habit, says that willpower "isn't just a skill. It's a muscle, like the muscles in your arms or legs, and it gets tired as it works harder, so there's less power left over for other things."

Change isn't going to happen by itself, but you don't necessarily need to make huge adjustments. Baby steps will get you there too and often make for more sustainable change. Study your heroes and discover the techniques they have used in their own lives. Often those who seem highly successful have put in a great deal of work to reach that point. We're often told not to copy others, to just be "ourselves," but attempting to copy others means learning from them. As writer Nicholas Delbanco once said, "To engage in imitation is to begin to understand what originality means."

Remember though, as you're embarking on your mission to "change" or "improve," that progress, not perfection, is the goal. Your aim should be to learn and to grow as you journey through life, rather than suddenly be a different person. It's also vital to remember that you can accept yourself as you are *and* desire to be better. The two states of mind are not mutually exclusive, and just because you'd like to grow, does not mean you need to punish your current self. In Pope St. Pius X's Worker's Prayer to

St. Joseph, this is referred to as avoiding vain complacency in success.

Most importantly, remember that this journey of change and growth you embark on – *this* is the part that people will attach to when you tell your business story. Your ability to understand and tell this narrative dictates if people root for you. People invest in people, not businesses. From investors to customers to employees – if you want to attract them to your business, you need to attract them to you simultaneously. If your story about how you became you is exciting and relatable, then an audience will be invested. It's all well to be "perfect," but if you arrive at that point too quickly, with no journey along the way or story to tell, then you'll face a much greater challenge selling yourself and your business to the world.

As your business continues to grow, it will certainly test your limits, and you will discover new boundaries and defining moments. Your patience, your intelligence, your intuition, your compassion ... all these things will change as you succeed, fail, make money, lose money, make friends, make enemies, be surprised, disappointed – basically all the ups and downs of human life. As you ride out these changes, you will begin to detach from the brand you have built your business around. Sometimes the brand will follow your identity, other times a divide will linger. Whatever the case, it's essential to understand the history, evolution, and challenges faced in the world of business branding, and how this well-trodden path will impact your entrepreneurial journey. The biggest four questions of your life build the strongest foundation for a lasting venture.

---

1. Michelle Obama, quoted in "HRH the Duchess of Sussex Interviews Michelle Obama in the September Issue," *vogue.co.uk*, July 30, 2019, Accessed: https://www.vogue.co.uk/article/michelle-obama-duchess-of-

sussex-interview-2019?fbclid=IwAR3c6qVzMDRhTTSqW--
xUJ6nYSDXlxzo41PqKdO6qJZ89s5GeBZNS55FuNU
2. Eric B. & Rakim "As The Rhyme Goes On" https://genius.com/Eric-b-and-
rakim-as-the-rhyme-goes-on-lyrics
3. Simon Moore, quoted in Kate Hilpern, "Who Made Me What I Am?", *The
Independent*, August 30, 2011, Accessed: https://www.independent.co.uk/
life-style/health-and-families/features/who-made-me-what-i-am-
2345823.html
4. https://storyshots.tumblr.com/post/25032057278/22-storybasics-ive-
picked-up-in-my-time-at-pixar
5. "The Autobiography of Gucci Mane." By Gucci Mane and Neil Martinez-
Belkin

CHAPTER 5

BRANDS

THE BLURRED LINE ~~between~~
Person and Business

If you've ever steered clear of a Saddleback caterpillar after seeing its vivid green corset, then you know the power of a personal brand. The Saddleback's distinctive stripe is a natural reminder to potential predators: "I'm poisonous, don't you think you'd be better off ordering pizza?"

If all those little caterpillar reps out there have done their jobs properly, then you'll already know what the bright green waistcoat stands for when you see it, and be able to say "hey you know what? This isn't for me." Brands are powerful like that, and this spins in the opposite direction too. Apples, for example, have developed those beautiful red hues, which, for thousands of years, have successfully enticed travelers to stop and collect fruit as a tasty road-trippin' snack. In the process, the seeds from the delicious apples are dispersed, and the plant has successfully used its unique "brand" to achieve a business goal: grow their business with little baby apple trees.

Of course this isn't a result of agency on the part of apple trees. A series of genetic mutations over many years led to success, but things could just as easily have gone the other way. The point here is: branding is everywhere and has been, in some form or another, for as long as there has been variety and competition on this earth. If you think you are exempt from needing to distinguish yourself in the world, then you are very much mistaken. The question is not whether you need a personal brand, but rather, how to build one in a genuine, meaningful, and impactful way.

Your key concern when developing your personal brand is *identity*. In order to have others identify with you, your brand must be *identifiable*. And in order to be identifiable, it must demonstrate *distinctiveness*. Character, upbringing, family, religion, physicality, interests, ethics, language, culture: these (and many more) are all building blocks of distinction, and it is from this pool of markers that your personal brand is built. Let's talk about Allbirds, a footwear company founded recently in 2014 that managed to capture a significant portion of the market in no time — a credit to their strong brand story that resonated with the customers. The brand story centers around their mission to create environment-friendly yet comfortable shoes, providing consumers with a better alternative to traditional footwear. While their brand identity is characterized by simplicity, sustainability, and innovation. The brand identity is also shaped by their transparency about sourcing materials and their dedication to reducing carbon emissions. But the intriguing question is, there are several brands doing the same, what's different? Along with the use of natural and renewable material, innovation and comfort, the minimalist designs, mid-range price point and transparency give them a competitive edge (differentiation) over the rivals.

In this chapter we look at the rise of the personal brand and its place in the contemporary business environment. I'll explain how desire for authenticity ultimately gave birth to the personal branding era, what the pitfalls of a personal brand done wrong can be (hint: undermining authenticity can ironically be one of them), and what you can do to get yours right.

The Banal History

Most of us know that the hot metal thing used to scorch a farmer's unique mark on a cow's keister is called a brand. Even more of us know that the names, symbols and other features of a given product are, collectivity, also known as brand. What we rarely acknowledge is the connection between this most simple form of cattle branding, and the more modern – developed by two hundred marketers after two hundred meetings – world of branding. In essence they are the same. The brand on a cow's ass is a unique stamp that says: "this is my cow, part of my farm." It makes the cow recognizable – distinct from others. At its heart, this is exactly what a more complex, business-based brand also sets out to achieve. Ownership. Distinction. Recognition.

Livestock owners have been branding their cattle since 2000 BC. The word "brand" dates back to the Old Norse "brand," and originally meant a piece of burning wood. By the time it reached late Middle English, it had become a verb, meaning – as it does today – to mark permanently with a hot iron. Branding in an even more basic form has been around for a lot longer, with marks, stamps and labels all used to denote maker or owner from Qin Dynasty China to Ancient Egypt.

In 12th century England, bakers and goldsmiths were required by the state to print personal brands on their loaves and metals – the association forcing each business owner to keep honest about their products' quantity. By 1618, the connection between brand and quantity had stretched to brand and *quality*, with an owner manufacturing high-quality cloth even taking a competitor to court for using the same stamp on their lesser-grade fabric.

It was in this context that mass branding emerged, a product of the Industrial Revolution and the changing face of manufacturing and distribution. Consumers, used to buying local products from local producers, were loyal to their village traders and wary of generic, mass-produced goods from further afield. Those out-of-town businesses (craft beer industry for example) came to understand very quickly that a generic product would have difficulty finding a market when the local population preferred familiar, locally-produced goods.

Factories, aware of customers' distrust, began painting logos onto the crates and barrels that held their products, slowly creating brand awareness among the wary village folk. It wasn't long either, before individual goods began to receive their own brands, and thus began the evolution of brands, switching from a focus on ownership to an emphasis on quality.

This major change in marketplace and business strategy gave rise to a new era of product branding, and soon made it to the US, paving the way for a range of products we continue to buy this day, including Coca-Cola, Campbell's Soup, and Juicy Fruit gum.

The "telling" of brands like these began in earnest in the early 20th century, largely thanks to Thomas J. Barratt, aka "the father of modern advertising," chairman of the Pears soap company. Barratt introduced a new advertising campaign using targeted slogans like "Good morning. Have you used Pears' soap?" which was well-known for many years. Soap companies like Pears also began to sponsor radio drama series, creating a new genre known as the "soap opera", and taking the promotion of brands to new heights.

While modern branding and business storytelling began in earnest in this era, it wasn't until around the 1950s that companies saw the need to give their products an identity to set them apart from the pack. Before that time, all you needed to do to ship goods was ... (drumroll) ... *make good ones*. With more and more competition came the need to dial up the promotion. When big name companies like Unilever and Procter and Gamble began noticing in the 1950s that their superior products were no longer so markedly superior than their competitors, they began to pay more attention to developing and managing their brand – giving their products a distinctive identity in an increasingly crowded marketplace.

With this, the "Mad Men" era was heralded in – the pioneering days of competitive advertising and the hard-working, hard-playing ad man of Madison Avenue. These were the creative years – when brands began to market based on fun, humor and irreverence, and sought for the first time that lucrative youth market. Advertising was on the nose, sexist, and ethically questionable – but the genius of its creators helped throw brand competition to even greater heights.

In 1984, the brand landscape changed again with Apple – the little computer start-up that could. Apple launched its Macintosh computer with the "1984" advertisement, screened during the Super Bowl. The ad, a $1.5 million-dollar blockbuster, directed by Ridley Scott, is considered a watershed moment in Apple's success as a business. Rather than focusing on the product from the outset, it told a story of breaking free from conformity, only showing the Mac in the final seconds of the advertisement. The strategy of Apple's marketers changed the face of branding and heralded a new era of business storytelling – one that appealed to emotions, to narrative, and which imbued inanimate objects with a sense of personality.

Just a few years later, the very concept of the brand was threatened by "Marlboro Friday" – still spoken about in hushed tones by the 1993 marketing biz alumni. Tobacco giant Philip Morris's decision to cut its prices by 20 percent under intense competition from generic brands sent the company's stock into freefall, and with it the whole stock market. Experts labeled Marlboro Friday "the death of brands." It was not.

<hr />

Ad Men

Ads suck. No one knows that more than the consumers. Gone are the days when people accepted a woman in an apron grimacing over a pair of bleached socks or allowed a tobacco company to tell them cigarettes are "the taste expectant mothers crave." The more creative brand managers have become (and they have become very, very creative), the more the brands themselves have begun to jump the shark, lose credibility, and alienate consumers.

Customers are also becoming more difficult to market to. Most of us have grown with the advertising industry, and we're wiser than ever to their cunning. We're now acutely aware of the tricks and traps of advertisers, and of the campaigners behind a campaign. As Stephen Brown, a professor of marketing research at the University of Ulster puts it:

...how can marketers market to marketing-savvy consumers when every conceivable combination of inclusion, nostalgia, and irony has already been attempted (as in Campbell Soup's "Just like Mother Used to Heat") and when marketers' increasingly common claims to authenticity, such as "Coca-Cola... Real," are patently preposterous, possibly ironic?[1]

We've moved on from the wild, pre-feminist Mad Men era to that of the "authentic" brand, however, authentic can sometimes mean anything but. In January 2019, razor company Gillette found that out the hard way when trying to get on the bandwagon of the #MeToo movement with their "The Best Men Can Be" advertisement. The slick two-minute video implores men to be less violent, less harassing, less condescending, less *masculine* – to become more gentle, more empathetic, more empowering of women. Unfortunately for Gillette, though no one can sustain a good argument *for* domestic violence, the moral imperative went down like a cup of cold sickness. Men revolted at being told their masculinity was toxic. Loyal customers swore off the brand. In August, Gillette's parent company Procter and Gamble took an $8 billion write-off for the brand, largely thanks to that campaign. (Also because everyone has hipster beards now and no need for razors. But that's another story.)

The point is: authenticity is hard. What's authentic to you, what comes from your heart, may still be perceived as fake by somebody else. It's therefore no longer enough to just "be you". When it comes to developing your personal brand, *be you,* but do it strategically, bearing in mind how you will be perceived by others. As Stephen Brown points out: "Authentic authenticity, so to speak, is unattainable."[2]

Previous generations of consumers were conscious of a brand's price, but in the current era are more and more concerned with the social and environmental impact of brands. Customers want to buy from companies that align with their own ethics and values and are willing to pay more to those brands who fit the bill. With the current climate change (pun intended), if a company so much as *thinks* about utilizing plastic bags, micro beads, disposable straws or ticker tape, they face enough public backlash to threaten decades of brand-building and consumer goodwill. These customer revolts have businesses under the thumb of consumers – quite a stark contrast to the business/customer relations of yore.

Contemporary brands are therefore forced to practice "proper" authenticity. Advertising can no longer risk bending the truth. Values can no longer be sidestepped. Apologies must be heartfelt. According to Stephen Brown, this is shifting the brand world to the fact-based storytelling of yesteryear:

Weary of asinine customer hug-a-thons and analogous brand-bonding brouhahas, consumers increasingly appreciate the honesty of up-front, forthright, show-me-the-money sales pitches. Today's customers are cognizant that underneath all the servile, sanctimonious, socially responsible rhetoric, marketing boils down to selling stuff. Good old-fashioned flimflam doesn't insult their marketing-savvy intelligence, whereas customer-coddling canoodling from the inclusive, I-will-always-love-you school of relationship marketing is increasingly treated with the contempt it deserves, as are nostalgia a-go-go and post-ironic posturing.[3]

You®

Being able to livestream wedding proposals on Facebook and threaten nuclear war via Twitter is all part of the magic of our digital Brave New World. While the internet has had a far-reaching impact on the way we live our lives, one of the more interesting effects has been on business, what is considered a business, and how businesses tell their stories. Companies' marketing platforms increasingly speak to us in the first person and exude a distinctive "best buds" personality. This shift – from shouting to conversing – has had a major effect on the brandification of people.

The idea of personal branding emerged in the late 1990s. Marketers David McNally and Karl Speak wrote in their 1999 book *Be Your Own Brand* that: "Your brand is a perception or emotion, maintained by somebody other than you, that describes the total experience of having a relationship with you".[4] Fast forward twenty years, and personal branding is a hot-property concept, with personally-branded personal branders lining up at the doors of entrepreneurs and pitching to personally present their own personal brands for a price.

Personal brands once had a more ... sinister tone. Slaves, gypsies, and the homeless have all been subjected to identifying marks through history. Nowadays the idea of a "personal brand" has all but replaced having a strong resume. More than this, it has replaced having a real *job*. If you are anything like me, your social media feeds are filled with pseudo life and business coaches, all telling you in descriptive, narrative ways why you should spend $29.99 and buy their "Six Steps to Social Media Success" business template. "Now Ross," you might rightly protest, "you've just spent the last four chapters telling us to tell our business story." That is indeed true. When everybody does it in the same way, however, in the same voice, and selling the same idea ... well, we start to turn off.

When I traveled to Southeast Asia, the same thing perplexed me, albeit in real life form. On the streets of Ho Chi Minh City, hawkers would pick a section of street to cover. Smart business tactic, you might argue. The problem was – everybody on that one street would sell the same thing. Sunglasses, for example. Everyone on the next street would sell decorative fans. You'd be so sick of having sunglasses shoved in your face by the end of the street, there's no way you'd consider buying a pair. Now yes, such retail clustering can have a justifiable application when it comes to stores, but in this context it just didn't make sense. It felt like all the locals had all only recently heard that tourists like sunglasses. Then they got their hands on some knock-off Ray-Bans and all decided to hang around the same neighborhood waiting for squinting, sun-dazzled Americans to come and find them.

The current trend of "I am my business" is the Western world's version of sunglasses street. Everyone is selling themselves online as a "marketing expert," a "business coach," a "social media guru." My favorites are the swathes of 20-year-old life coaches out there telling us: "Let your smile change the world, but don't let the world change your smile." When a 20-year-old who has never held down a real job tries to sell us career advice ... we know something's askew in the authenticity stakes. As Will Reynolds has written for Virgin's *Entrepreneur* blog:

For many, the idea of a personal brand is an unwelcome extension of the perceived superficiality of marketing, and suggests the kind of bogus outward appearance that one might expect from a sugary drink telling us that consuming its contents is tantamount to living happily ever after.[5]

That's not to say that social media isn't a viable place to market yourself as a consultant or coach. Be aware though, how saturated the market is with personal brands, and consider how you can make yourself stand out from the crowd. Whatever your niche, remember that your brand should never be a coffin. It's not a box, and you do not need to live and die by it. The best-case scenario, in fact, is building up your brand, then eventually shedding that skin and taking on a life of your own. Let's call it post-brand metamorphism. Fly, you beautiful butterfly.

In short, if you're a nutrition coach and want to eat cookies for breakfast ... eat cookies for breakfast. If you're a life coach that loves spending whole weekends playing Playstation ... then play Playstation. Don't hide your quirks. Embrace them, and your audience will love you all the more for it. As Will Reynolds writes: "the power of a well crafted digital persona should be ignored at your own risk."[6]

Fifteen Minutes of Shame

One thing never changes in the history of business: the consumer is always the judge and the jury. That has never been more true than in this day and age, when personal brands can be sent to hell in a hand basket by a vengeful consumer base. Case in point: in May 2019, author Natasha Tynes fires off a tweet showing a DC Metro worker eating on the train. The backlash begins almost immediately and escalates rapidly. Tynes is called racist, a snitch, and receives death threats for the tweet. An author and self-proclaimed social media "strategist", she is abandoned by her publisher, and flees the US to her native Jordan to escape the vitriol. Any personal brand she has built up over her professional career is swept away in a flash flood. Deserving of such vehement opposition or not, Tynes' case demonstrates the enormous power of Joe Public to make or break a person's business by finding a hole in their character.

Another unfortunate case was with Justine Sacco. She was the top PR person for InterActiveCorp. Before boarding an 11-hour flight to South Africa, she tweeted: "Going to Africa. Hope I don't get AIDS. Just kidding. I'm white!"[7] This tweet was picked up by Sam Biddle at Valleywag and went viral while she was on her flight. The incident launched a hashtag, #HasJustineLandedYet. Upon landing, she found that her tweet had caused a significant backlash, leading to her being fired from her job. She later apologized for her "needless and careless tweet" about AIDS in Africa.

This level of personal backlash is a relatively new phenomenon. Previously, it was big business that attracted such big opposition. Now a relatively minor personal slip-up can lead to total character annihilation. Composer and comedian Tim Minchin references this in his song "15 Minutes":

In the future,
Everyone will have
15 minutes
15 minutes of shame
15 minutes where they
Are unforgivable
Irredeemable
Inexcusable scum.[8]

Notwithstanding the similarly titled piece of literature, there are no long shades of gray when it comes to representations of character. You're a Nobel Prize winning humanitarian who adopts puppies from war zones? That's all very nice but two months ago you called a woman "sweetheart" in a moment of sarcastic douchebaggery and now the *entire world hates you and wishes you a painful death.* We have lost the ability to scale our outrage, and as a result entrepreneurs must take note: the fall from a well-built personal brand can be a painful one, regardless of how high or low the dive.

Although falls from grace can be random or over-exaggerated, it still pays to set yourself up for success. Pick your language carefully. As Liz Ryan warns us in "The Six Worst

Ways to Brand Yourself," words like "savvy, strategic, expert, or visionary" should be used with care, and "mogul, maven, guru, authority, or specialist" shouldn't be touched with a ten-foot barge pole.[9] Using these terms only serves to tell your audience that you have empty words. "Zombie language" like "thinking outside the box" and "blue sky thinking" is similarly problematic – a type of business-speak that has a special place in personal branding hell and is impersonal, trite, and utterly fails to describe who you are.

Ryan also identifies "trophy speak" as a must to avoid:

"Ivy League grad and alum of Apple, Google and Snap." Now you've made it clear that you were able to get into an Ivy League school and that you subsequently worked for Apple, Google and Snap. All that tells us is that these three organizations (four if we count the Ivy League college) found you acceptable for their needs.[10]

The last deadly branding mistake, Ryan contends, "is to call yourself a Disruptor, a Change Agent or a Catalyst" – all these scream "cliché" and reek of inauthenticity.

Don't make the mistake of thinking that you gain a business advantage by manipulating your image in order to form a more 'likable' personal brand and using language like that outlined by Ryan. Stephen Covey, author of the well-known book "The 7 Habits of Highly Successful People" calls this the "personality ethic", explained here by Will Reynolds:

The underlying assumption of the Personality Ethic is that who you are matters less than who people think you are. A slick website and consistent flow of content, even an impressive portfolio, may well boost an individual's short-term advantage. But style without substance is an unsustainable strategy, and an outside-in approach focusing on personality before character often results in long-term frustration for both the individual and employer.[11]

As Reynolds goes on to contend, this age of the personal brand is breeding distrust – something business storytellers must be aware of and take steps to mitigate:

The mismatch between the expectations set by a well honed personal brand, and the reality of somebody's effectiveness, is an increasingly evident phenomenon. With a growing contingent workforce, the dark side of the moon is that some workers become short-termist in their approach, relying too heavily on their outward appearance for short-term success. Oftentimes the net effect of this is an erosion of trust, and a lack of confidence that people are who they appear to be.[12]

The Un-Brand is On-Brand

You *can* be a life coach who eats cookies for breakfast. You can be an eco-warrior who occasionally forgets their coffee cup. You can be you – and equipped with answers to the four big life questions of the previous chapter, you can be you without getting stuck in a mold. There are two key things to be aware of before you start out:

1. Set the expectation where it feels right, not where you think it should be.

2. Understand and embrace the complexity of you so others can too.

The world is getting sick of branded people. We're dying for some real-life authenticity, nothing scripted, nothing filtered, nothing perfect. So be the Saddleback caterpillar and show your true colors. Don't make the parameters of your personal brand so rigid that you have no room to change or develop. Set out to be who you are and your brand will naturally mature. When you inevitably metamorphize, as we all do, nobody can argue that you went from caterpillar to moth overnight. The joy is in the journey, and people (even as brands) will always have a more exciting and engaging path than a product or service.

---

1. Stephen Brown, "Marketing to Generation®", *Harvard Business Review*, June 2003, Accessed: https://hbr.org/2003/06/marketing-to-generation
2. Ibid.
3. Ibid.
4. David McNally & Karl Speak, *Be Your Own Brand*, (San Francisco, Berrett-Koehler Publishers, 2002) p.4.
5. Will Reynolds, "Personal Branding: The good, the bad and the undeniable", *Virgin.com*, November 16, 2015, Accessed: https://www.virgin.com/entrepreneur/personal-branding-good-bad-and-undeniable
6. Ibid.
7. https://uproxx.com/viral/what-happened-to-justine-sacco-the-woman-whose-life-was-ruined-by-an-aids-joke-she-made-on-twitter/
8. Tim Minchin, "15 minutes of Shame", Accessed: https://www.youtube.com/watch?v=ePsWowEtKt8
9. Liz Ryan, "The Six Worst Ways to Brand Yourself", *Forbes.com*, March 23, 2017, Accessed: https://www.forbes.com/sites/lizryan/2017/03/23/the-six-worst-ways-to-brand-yourself/#52a0a91c3c59
10. Ibid.
11. Reynolds, "Personal Branding: The good, the bad and the undeniable."
12. Ibid.

CHAPTER 6

AUTHENTICITY IN THE RED LIGHT DISTRICT

HOW TO AVOID GETTING CAUGHT
with Your Pants Down

Only the truth of who you are, if realized, will set you free.

ECKHART TOLLE

We're not in a scene from Gladiator, so the above line from author and quote-factory Eckhart Tolle is a bit dramatic. Still, he makes a valid point. The reason you do what you do stems from the core of who you are. At a certain point, who you are will challenge who you feel you are destined to be. Indeed, your whole life is a Bermuda Triangle of who you claim to be, others' perceptions of you, and that wonderful, slippery thing called the truth.

We live in an age of sell-outs. I don't mean that quite as superciliously as it sounds, it's simply a fact of the modern era. We live in an age of sell-outs, and because of this, we are often terrified of selling out. This is a hard road to navigate. Life is prodigiously more complex than it was one hundred years ago. Today, we're faced with all manner of decisions and compromises – not all of which we're comfortable with, but many of which we deem necessary – politically, economically, socially, romantically, and morally. Many of us have danced with the devil, if only to keep him at arm's length. Of course, the devil is subjective – for you, it may be the wrong side of a moral issue, working in a field you don't agree with, or overlooking behavior you find repugnant. Whatever your compromise, you've likely sold out at some stage of your life, and that's *okay*. I'd be blown away if you hadn't sold off part of yourself for the greater good of your cause. That's not what this is about. The goal of articulating your true self is actually to eliminate the idea of selling, as we'll explore later.

Authenticity is all about being *real*. Up until about 2010, authenticity was used in the context of something not being fake. *Is this Louis Vuitton purse authentic?* In this chapter we look at bigger-picture authenticity, and how to avoid prostituting yourself as you fight to get your name out there into the world. We'll look at the changing expectations of consumers around honesty and authenticity, the psychology of how we interact with brands, the existential imperative to *grow*, the importance of being earnest – in both achievement and maintenance – and, for those times when it all goes pear-shaped, why it's so vitally important to say "sorry."

Exposing Yourself

We're a suspicious bunch, us humans. We harbor an inherent distrust of people trying to sell to us. Yet advertising is all around us – we wade through an ocean of it every year. In 2017, the average American consumer was exposed to between

4,000 and 10,000 brand messages every single day.[1] In the 1970s, that was just 500 per day.[2]

A report from 2017 by Trinity Mirror, a publisher and Ipsos, a market researcher points to rapidly declining trust in advertising and brands. 42% of survey participants claimed to distrust brands – making suspicion the baseline for brand-consumer relationships.[3] That's a hard starting point to be faced with as a corporation, let alone an entrepreneur going it alone.

The stats get even worse when we narrow the demographic. A report from 2015 by a marketing and strategy firm The McCarthy Group found that 84% of millennials don't trust traditional advertising.[4] For instance, in the '80s, PepsiCo rolled out the iconic "Pepsi Challenge" advertising campaign. They conducted blind taste tests to show that people preferred the taste of Pepsi over Coca-Cola. This campaign was a classic example of traditional advertising through television and print media. However, when PepsiCo revisited this campaign in 2011, they encountered significant skepticism from millennials, who had become a dominant consumer group by then. Millennials were known for valuing authenticity and were more likely to question marketing claims. Thus, PepsiCo decided to re-launch this campaign, this time adding digital and social media elements. They encouraged millennials to share their unscripted, real-time reactions to blind taste tests on platforms like YouTube, Facebook, and Twitter. Participants were given control over the content they shared, adding an element of authenticity to the campaign.

This distrust of social media has changed the way we consume content, newspapers, TV, and radio ads. As a Marketing Strategist and Huffington Post contributor Matthew Tyson points out:

In 20 years of using the Internet, I don't think I've ever clicked on a banner ad. In my house, sales papers go to either the trash or the fireplace. Right now, as I write this, Spotify just interrupted my playlist of instrumental concentration music to play an ad, and I have no idea what that ad was about.[5]

Tyson's not alone. We just don't like being sold anymore. We suspect someone of trying to take our money, change our opinion, or influence us, and we balk. That's why the game has changed. Brands are no longer sexy, emotionally manipulative, big-budget beasts shouting at us. They're our friends, our role models, our Instagram buddies. The essence of "brand" has undergone a monumental shift since the dawn of the social media era, and with that shift has come changes in the rules of the game.

Nobody questions the mandate of traditional advertising campaigns. You don't see an ad for Coca-Cola on the television and go nuts because they're adding vanilla orange peel to the formula. Yet this is increasingly the reaction to personal brands who are seen to be stepping outside their "authentic selves" and selling something. UK-based blogger Scarlett London found this out the hard way when, in 2018, she posted a standard Instagram post featuring a bit-too-perfect, pretty in-pink scene, which had been sponsored by mouthwash brand Listerine. The post – a relatively innocuous piece of social media gloss – went viral, and London received a flash flood of scorn and death threats. The post, it seems – just one in a sea of far more explicit advertisements – was considered inauthentic. While London had tagged the photo to indicate it was a paid post, her followers revolted against what seemed like an overly glossy portrayal of everyday life.[6]

Matthew Tyson describes the new relationship between brands and audiences as being "like two parents harassing their daughter's new boyfriend," explaining that "millennials need to know you before they'll trust you. They want transparency. They want brands to interact. Simply put, they want to know we're dealing with real humans, not faceless corporations."[7] Everlane, for example, has made transparency a core part of its business model after recognizing it as one of the crucial factors to win the customer's heart. The brand proudly displays all the costs of production including labor, transportation, and overheads with the information accessible to customers on their website. They offer virtual tours of their production units with insights into their factory partners, working conditions and shoot locations. Everlane is one of the champions advocating ethical sourcing and they go the extra mile by disclosing the environmental impact of their products. In doing so, they empower customers with the knowledge they need to make informed and conscious choices.

I'm a bit hesitant to buy-in on the total transparency track, as it isn't the main component of authenticity, but it is most certainly a major element of handling your progression. Whatever your own opinion of the key tenets of authenticity, understanding audiences' perceptions of brands should be your starting point for ensuring your brand is built on a firm foundation of reality.

Loose Change

You are not a single picture. You are worth well over 1,000 words, and your life has highs, lows, and HD 8K technicolor (maybe some blurry parts too). You are not even a painting, so you are going to change. Likewise, the environment you're operating within changes too. The most successful personal brands are those that move both with their masters and the spinning of the earth.

It's not just that you will change, it's that you *should* change. Not necessarily in monumental ways, but in considerate, educated, growth-centered ways. Your authentic self is a never-ending evolution, not a destination. Why do you do what you do? As you ask yourself why you want to be like your idols, not like them, and where you see yourself in them, you should similarly ask yourself: When am I my happiest? When do I like being myself? When do I hate being myself? What version of myself do I want to bring out more often? This is some seriously introspective malarkey, but the more you understand it, the less you'll need to *sell* yourself. The more you recognize your evolution and why you are doing what you're doing (whether admirable or tyrannical), the less room for distrust there will be.

To be authentic, your brand needs to be malleable. To be malleable, you need to set it up right. If you come right out of the gate twirling your lasso and hollering that you hate vegetables, then it's going to be way harder to do an about-face later when you marry the heir to a pea farm. A better approach acknowledges the inherent complexity of the human character: "Hi, I'm Marty. I'm a businessman and a father, and I'm not great at eating my vegetables." Later on, you can take your audience along on your change journey with you: "Remember when I said I don't like vegetables? Well, I've made my peace with peas, and want to share a recipe with y'all that made me see the light."

This isn't to say that you should avoid opinions, shy away from taking a stand, or avoid being a specialist. You should do all those things. Just don't fence yourself in. At the end of the day, your business should be a mirror and a learning opportunity –

not just the world around you but also yourself. With any learning opportunity comes the need for a degree of humility. Don't act in fear of how your future self will view your current self, but be mindful of how you may evolve with maturity and education.

A Five-Step Reality Check

If I tell you that I'm authentic, does that invalidate my authenticity? When reaching a fork in the road, you'll meet plenty of others who likely know better than you. The problem is, as poet Henry Wadsworth Longfellow once noted: "We judge ourselves by what we feel capable of doing, while others judge us by what we have already done."[8] This means that with any change, there will be an element of proving yourself involved. So long as you're authentic in what you do and say, you should have no trouble showing that you are justified in taking a place at that particular table.

It's hard to advise about authenticity. Ultimately, the genuineness of your relationships comes down to you and is not something that can be rehearsed in the mirror. There are steps you can take to hold yourself accountable in the authenticity stakes. Self-reflection is key in the brand-building world, so if you do anything – set aside some time every few months to consider where your brand has come from and where it's going. Think about whether or not the person you're projecting is still the person you are and follow these tips to staying on the authenticity track.

- Communicate your roots and stay true to them.

For better or worse, our formative years shaped us into the people we are today. Often that's the aspect of someone's personality we're most interested in discovering. Oh, you're sailing around on a private yacht in Croatia chugging Dom Perignon? That's very nice, but how did you get there? What shaped you as a person? Where is *home* to you?

- Use stories, not jargon.

You have idioms. That's great. But for the love of laundry lists, prime your audience with a summary so they won't be bored stiff reading about another #influencer #growthhacker #digitalnomad #entrepreneur who is #passionate #driven #successful #sought after. What customers truly crave are the stories telling "How" & "Why" aspects of the journeys. If you can provide an example, it pumps the tank with credibility.

- Listen

If you're a real-life person with a real-life business then you'll have real-life customers. Customers are the lifeblood of your business, and without them, everything you do loses meaning. What's my point? Shut up and listen. Imbuing your brand with conversational power gives you a good share of authenticity. If you simply use your soapbox to shout at people, they're not going to relate to you as much as if you involve them, listen to them, and make them feel valued.

- Be real, not #blessed.

Look, I get it. Sunsets on tropical beaches are awesome. Business class flights are awesome. Resort spa treatments are awesome. This may well be your real day-to-day life, in which case – awesome! Even if it is, practice a little humility, show a little vulnerability, and don't pretend you're invincible. Your saturated images may attract plenty of followers, but if you don't share little nuggets of your real life, or real character from time to time, then you won't hold their attention forever.

- Be transparent.

Are you struggling with something this week? Are big changes coming? Are you partnering up with a new investor? There's an art to openness, and baring your soul is not necessarily the best idea, but if you don't let your customers in – at least a little – they'll feel excluded and accuse you of hiding something. I can't overstate the benefits of a little "behind the scenes" storytelling to boost the authenticity factor of your business. You can balance transparency and privacy, its equal and opposite force.

Vulnerability is Your Superpower

Everyone has vulnerabilities. Sometimes, though, when you see your friends, acquaintances, and idols beaming at you from some tropical beach via social media – it's easy to think: *That's so great. Their life is so great.* Then you start to wonder how reflective their avatar is of who they are. In one image, we can feel admiration, jealousy, doubt, depression, hope, and more. We all have peaks and valleys on this human journey so if you're projecting an image that has none, it's unlikely people will find you genuine. If somebody says their life is perfect, they're lying. That's not to say a healthy dose of positivity doesn't imbue life with a rosy glow, but regardless of how content you are – something in your life is, or has been, tough.

To be able to communicate our vulnerabilities takes honesty and nerves of steel. I'm not suggesting that you spill your tell-all to every stranger, but you have permission to take your audience a little past the facade. But how? Narrate your struggles, acknowledge/admit your mistakes, voice social issues, highlight employee stories and accept uncertainty. Story Time! Blue Bell Creameries, a well-loved Texas based ice cream brand, faced a significant vulnerability in 2015 when its products were linked to listeria - a dangerous bacterium that can cause serious illness. Multiple cases of listeriosis were reported, including several hospitalizations and three tragic deaths.The outbreak not only severely threatened the brand's reputation but also the trust of the consumers, potential legal liability from affected individuals and families and significant financial losses. The company's operations were closely scrutinized for compliance with food safety regulations which further led to job uncertainty among the employees.

Blue Bell took immediate and appropriate steps to handle the situation, some critics might not agree with me. However, The brand openly communicated with the public using various media platforms, implemented rigorous new safety procedures, included extensive testing with a commitment to meeting or exceeding industry standards. The CEO and company leadership publicly apologized for the outbreak and expressed deep sorrow for the individuals affected. They took full responsibility for the situation. Accepting the vulnerability helped the company to regain the lost trust, rebuild the brand image and strengthen the relationship with the loyal customers.

But why? To know a little about your vulnerabilities means to understand the depth of your character. Any audience armed with that knowledge will feel more inclined to connect with you, your business, and your message.

Vulnerability is, unfortunately, not taught in school (especially not in business school). To be vulnerable, you've got to be willing to let go a little. Not everyone will like you. Sometimes, you won't even like you. As you grow and experience ups and downs, the only essential part is negating the urge to discount your emotions. You do not need a certain degree of disappointment for it to be valid. You do not need a certain degree of success to celebrate.

Putting yourself out there, facing opposition, and continuing anyway – that's the power of vulnerability. This is what helps us stay authentic. We dump on YouTube stars who open boxes and make a few million dollars for it, but we're drawn to their vulnerability. We're drawn to the fact that they are putting their face out there for people to like and dislike regularly. Are you prepared to step out on the ledge like that? The difference between the people unboxing on camera and the people unboxing at home is their vulnerability.

As an entrepreneur, you are putting your creation, your service, and your likeness on display. You can read all the tips you like on how to be authentic or, even worse, *seem* authentic, but this is simple. Authenticity is vulnerability.

The Art of Saying Sorry

We have a real tough time admitting we're wrong, taking the time to understand it. We're never more vulnerable than when we make a mistake and have to face up to it. How we do that is telling. It's a test of our character and the moral foundation of our business. The art of humility is at the heart of an authentic brand, and if something goes wrong, you'll need to know when and why to say sorry.

Your code of ethics is derived from considering the Four Biggest Questions of your life, so you shouldn't find yourself in too much hot water to begin with. Your code of ethics is one of the most deeply personal things about you and not something you can learn from a book. You do have a code of ethics, even if you couldn't immediately write it down in a coherent way. You have been raised with certain principles – good or bad – and your friends, colleagues, and acquaintances have taught you, in words or actions, how to behave. You might use religion or politics as a guiding star for the way you move through life. Whatever the source, your code of ethics tells you: whether or not you're okay stealing an idea from a business partner, whether or not you should give away most of your income to charity, or whether or not you're willing to be sponsored by that big tobacco company.

If you're following this code, it should see you through your business without incident. But as Shakespeare once said, upon occasion excrement doth occureth. When that hits the proverbial fan, you're going to need to own up. Your code of ethics may have been flawed, or a reaction was unexpected, but there's generally only one way forward: genuine remorse.

Apologies are today's measure of whether people are authentic – whether or not they mean it – whatever "it" may be. The problem is that there's also a fervent apology that tends to tip authenticity on its head. It's a double-edged sword, and one you can only hope you don't have to navigate during your career.

Whether or not you agree with our culture of contrition or not, it exists, and for the most part, you'll need to operate within the social norms *du jour* (unless, of course, you're Tina Fey, who has "opted out" of the culture of demanding apologies).[9] Alexander Pope famously declared "To err is human." That is certainly true in the contemporary era, but with a caveat: to apologize is expected. Incongruent behavior served with a bit of *mea culpa* will no longer take you far in life. As we continue to face this apology epidemic and whatever evolution cancels culture takes, I encourage you to search for earnestness and awareness in all that you do.

————————————

1. Jon Simpson, "Finding Brand Success in the Digital World", *Forbes.com*, August 25, 2017, accessed: https://www.forbes.com/sites/forbesagencycouncil/2017/08/25/finding-brand-success-in-the-digital-world/#3bbc9f24626e

2. Caitlin Johnson, "Cutting Through Advertising Clutter", *cbsnews.com*, September 17, 2006, Accessed: https://www.cbsnews.com/news/cutting-through-advertising-clutter/

3. Andrew Tenzer & Hannah Chalmers, "When Trust Falls Down: How brands got here and what they need to do about it", *ipsos.com*, 2017, Accessed: https://www.ipsos.com/sites/default/files/2017-06/Ipsos_Connect_When_Trust_Falls_Down.pdf

4. The McCarthy Group, "Millennials: Trust and Attention Survey", 2014, Accessed: https://static1.squarespace.com/static/5c61c52811f78475c8a8a6c5/t/5c6c23f16e9a7f0b4e4ad353/1550590961706/millenial+survey.pdf

5. Matthew Tyson, "Millennials Want Brands To Be More Authentic. Here's Why That Matters," *Huffpost.com*, January 20, 2017, Accessed: https://www.huffpost.com/entry/millennials-want-brands-t_b_9032718

6. Rachel Hosie, "Blogger Mocked for Staged Instagram Post Reveals She's Received Death Threats", *independent.co.uk*, September 3, 2018, Accessed: https://www.independent.co.uk/life-style/scarlett-london-instagram-death-threats-blogger-twitter-viral-a8520311.html

7. Matthew Tyson, "Millennials Want Brands To Be More Authentic. Here's Why That Matters."

8.

9. Olivia Blair, "Tina Fey criticizes 'culture of demanding apologies' and claims she won't apologize if people find her jokes offensive", *independent.co.uk*, December 22, 2015, Accessed: https://www.independent.co.uk/news/people/tina-fey-criticises-culture-of-demanding-apologies-and-claims-she-wont-apologise-if-people-find-her-a6783101.html

CHAPTER 7

FRAMED THREE WAYS

THERE ARE, in effect, three elements to how your story can be framed: what people think, what you claim, and what is true. Two of these you can control and the jury will deliberate accordingly. While there is no pecking order to them, you are the sun that gives energy to all three. For example, you may claim that you are the fastest runner in Texas. People may look at you, watch you race, and think you are the fastest person in Texas. However, if you fall short at the state trials, then what is true has left you short of an authentic connection.

In the same light, you may be the fastest runner in the Lone Star state. People may think it, too, but if you don't claim it before the run begins then you've missed out on an opportunity to capture the audience. Your story, like every great story, can bring us along if you let it.

You win when what you claim and what people think is in line with what is true.

What People Think

Perception is a powerful element. Ignore its impact on your business at your peril. From a psychological perspective, perception describes how sense-based information is interpreted and experienced by the person receiving it.[1] Our perceptions are influenced by both bottom-up processing – how sensory inputs create the way we see things – as well as top-down processing – how our existing experiences and knowledge influence our interpretation of those sensations.[2]

Many inputs affect the way we perceive the world around us – attention is one of them. After a strenuous exam, for example, your classmate may complain about "how loud that clock was ticking!" while you heard nothing. In reality, your hearing is no worse than hers, but she heard and perceived the noise as an annoyance while you processed it differently. Beyond our senses, our experiences and our access to information all influence how we process someone else's story.

Culture, to the degree of diversity to which we've been exposed, correlates to how we see the world around us. A 1963 multinational study, for example, found that individuals living in Western countries were much more susceptible to specific kinds of visual illusions, such as the Müller-Lyer illusion, which shows two straight lines that can appear to be of differing lengths but are the same measurement.[3]

The authors of this study – Marshall Segall, Donald Campbell, and Melville Herskovits – found that those raised in non-Western cultures were less prone to experiencing the visual illusion and determined that this difference in perception corresponded to the differences in the kinds of environmental features experienced by people in those cultures. For example, individuals from Western countries are more accustomed to seeing buildings with straight lines: the study called this "a carpentered world." In certain non-Western cultures, however, individuals did not have this perception of straight lines, growing up, for example, in round huts arranged in a circle (in the case of the Zulu of South Africa).[4]

I want to also look at the environment. What people think has a direct correlation to where they are. Our surroundings set us up to behave, how we listen, our information retention, and more. Are you in a classroom? Are you in someone's home? Are you delivering a keynote at a Jamaican resort? These factors all lead to what people think, but that doesn't stay in their heads. What people think now surfaces in reviews. We now live in a reputation economy, and we have to bring awareness to the stories we tell and understand that where we tell it, both physically and by which medium, makes a difference.

Motivation also has a major impact on perception. If you've ever been expecting a delivery from Amazon, then you may imagine a doorbell ringing. Your brain anticipates the sound of footsteps on the path or a truck engine idling. If so, you've experienced the way motivation allows us to perceive information that isn't there.

Our personalities also have a huge impact on our perceptions in life. Children who have "thrill-seeker" personality traits are more likely to enjoy and seek out sour flavors, according to a 2004 study.[5] Another study found that individuals who have positive attitudes toward reduced-fat foods are more likely to rate such foods as tasting better than those who have less positive attitudes about such items.[6]

Other people will always view you differently thanks to the unique interaction between the wiring of their brain, their upbringing and culture, and the impressions you give off – intentionally or inadvertently. Sometimes people are going to walk in the door with a preconceived notion of you based on the side of the bed they got up on. How then can you, as an entrepreneur, influence and/or navigate the way others perceive your story?

Let's talk about Nike and its Pro Hijab Campaign (2017). This is an excellent example of how people from diverse backgrounds perceived the campaign in their unique ways. Bear in mind that the thought process of the Western and Muslim countries specifically is sizably different. The West is on the considered to be at the highest level of open-mindedness, and the Muslim world is still working on progressive values. Nike aimed to introduce a performance-oriented athletic headscarf for Muslim women athletes. In Western countries, this campaign was warmly welcomed, generally praised for its inclusivity, cultural sensitivity, and was perceived as a positive step towards recognizing Muslim women in sports. However, the campaign had mixed views from Middle Eastern and other Muslim countries. Some saw it as a positive step towards inclusivity and others perceived it as a challenge to established cultural norms. In some regions with conservative cultural norms, the Nike Pro Hijab campaign faced challenges and criticism. There were debates about whether the campaign was appropriate or if it undermined traditional values. Overall, the Nike Pro Hijab campaign had a global impact, with Muslim women athletes around the world expressing their appreciation for the product and the brand's recognition of their needs.

- Understand Visual Cues

There is no right or wrong way to look, but we all must accept that sometimes appearance matters. You eat with your eyes before your mouth, right? A stranger can form an opinion of you within 33 milliseconds of meeting.[7] This can happen even before you open your mouth. So, what's a surefire way to start on the right foot? Appearance!

This doesn't automatically equate to the clothes you wear – although NOT wearing clothes may narrow your opportunities depending on the business. Appearance is how you carry yourself and being intentional about it. The way you stand, the expression on your face, the eye contact, attention to detail, the length of your beard, the style of your hair, interactions with those around you, and your smile. You are in control of all these things, and to a significant extent you can craft a first impression by considering these to be tools at your disposal.

Sometimes, though, perceptions of presentation are out of your hands. If I walk into a job interview wearing an unbuttoned linen shirt dotted with flamingos, you're either going to think I'm a fun, bold, creative guy or that I'm rude and inappropriate. This perception of me is a mix of my behavior and the lens that another person is viewing me through. Sometimes there's no telling how the latter will pan out.

- Personality on Display

Put your personality at the forefront of your interactions. Show your true colors, don't assume they don't belong in business interactions. This comes back to putting authenticity at the heart of your business story. Don't expect that people will automatically see you for who you are. If you want to be perceived a certain way, then march your personality out front and center. If you put yourself in a position to be yourself and not be someone who is in a conversation to get something out of it, the relationship has a much better chance of lasting. Using your personality to add value, not extract it.

- Less Talk, More Rock

There's a funny thing about others' perceptions of you:

they're pretty sensitive to bullshit. You can strut your stuff, talk yourself up, and act bigger and bolder than you are – but in the end, people will almost always judge you based on your actions rather than your words.

So what? So focus on doing, not talking. Fancy yourself as a philanthropic soul? That's great, but don't tell everyone you are one before going out there and working in your local soup kitchen. And no, not just once. Do it every Sunday for a year and then, and only then, think about mentioning it in dispatches.

- Hanging with the right crowd

Short of sounds like an anti-drug ad, I'll say this one is simple math. You are the sum of your parts. If your confidants are confidence tricksters, phonies, or short-term thinkers, you'll always risk being tarred with the same brush. The company you keep tells the stories you'll reap. Are the five people you talk to the most challenging you or keeping you where you are?

What You Claim

You can and should find ways to claim your story. While this has some elements of PR or clickbait, that doesn't assume a negative connotation. However, this is the most hazardous part of storytelling. The Talented Mr. Ripley once said: "I always thought it'd be better to be a fake somebody than a real nobody." Fantasists and serial exaggerators often harbor a sense of inadequacy that speaks to Tom Ripley's quote. The pathological urge to remake oneself afresh is far from unique to fiction – impostors have long lurked in the halls of truth. During the Korean War, for example, a hospital orderly, Ferdinand Waldo Demara, stole the identity of naval surgeon Joseph Cyr. He managed to wing his way through many major surgeries, giving generous amounts of penicillin to his unsuspecting patients to smooth the way.

Demara's claim faced the ultimate test when a whopping sixteen Korean combat casualties were brought aboard his ship – several requiring major surgery. Ordering his colleagues to prepare the men, Demara proceeded to speed-read his textbook on general surgery, before emerging and performing major operations on the injured men – none of whom died as a result. Win! Of course, he was ultimately found out and spent the rest of his life running from the bad name he'd given himself. So ... not such a win after all.

Anna Sorokin, aka 'Anna Delvey' is a modern-day Ferdinand Demara and an excellent, semi-tragic example of an entrepreneur's claims gone absolutely round the bend. Sorokin – a young Russian woman – managed to convince scores of New York acquaintances that she was a wealthy German heiress with a hefty trust fund who intended to set up an arts foundation. Staying at luxury hotels and skipping the tab, eating at trendy restaurants and conveniently 'forgetting' her wallet, and generally weaving an incredible web of deceit, Sorokin was eventually arrested on six charges of grand larceny and sentenced to between four and twelve years in state prison.

What possessed her to do this? Sorokin's case is an extreme example of the divergence between a claim and the truth. Although the truth, as we'll discover below, is exceptionally hard to define, one key test is whether or not you believe, in your heart, that what you claim is true. In Sorokin's case, no matter how extreme her delusion, it seems likely that she knew she was lying.

Why did she continue down that path then? I'm not a psychologist, nor a criminal prosecutor. But what I see in the Anna Delvey/Sorokin case is a young woman with big ideas who so badly wanted to make them happen, that she *stepped outside of herself* to achieve them. Let's be clear – I'm not glorifying her actions. She committed crimes and was wholly unfeeling toward her victims. The divide though, between what she claimed, and what was true, was so vast, she fell into the chasm of her creation. 'Anna Delvey' was the ultimate entrepreneurial story. For a time it was perceived well by those around her until they realized just how incongruent her claims and the truth were.

What *should* you claim, then, if claims so easily descend into the untrue? First off, you can claim many things without feeling you are exaggerating, bragging, or lying. Claiming is about staking your place, asserting your right to present yourself to the world, and proudly announcing your expertise, talents and meaningful contributions to society. Claiming is not the equivalent of bragging. It's seeking recognition that is a vital practice as a business owner. Sara Blakely, the founder of Spanx, is the perfect example. She made big claims of helping different communities through her work and services over the years. Let's investigate and see if she's genuinely as good as she claims to be, or if she's just exaggerating or adding extra flair to her statements. First and foremost, Sara claims that she is an advocate for women's empowerment, and the idea for Spanx came from this very mission and (dramatic pause)... yes, it's true! Her products are designed to boost women's self-esteem and body confidence. Blakely has actively supported and mentored female entrepreneurs through various initiatives and programs like "Leg Up" to not only support financially but also mentor to start their own businesses.

The second big claim is charity, and it's true as well. Sara Blakely donated $5 million to support the Oprah Winfrey Leadership Academy for Girls in South Africa and pledged to donate $5 million amid COVID-19. Now, are there actually any advantages for a business owner when their claims are true?

Genuine claims help a business to improve its credibility, have competitive edge over its rivals, attract exceptional talent globally, investor appeal and most importantly customer loyalty by winning their hearts.

The Guinness Book of World Records is full of claims that have been acknowledged as truths. There's some pretty unbelievable stuff in that book – but what makes the claims legitimate is their verification by others. The perception of others (in this case, Guinness officials) that what they are seeing is true and real, and the claim of the record-setter that what they are doing is the fastest/biggest/wettest/highest/best – these two stars align and create a reality. Without convincing others in some legitimate way that their claims are believable, the Guinness Book of World Records would simply be a large tome full of crazy people arguing that they're the fastest person in the world at cutting nose hair or the person who can hang upside down by the callous on their big toe the longest. When you set out to tell your story, don't be afraid to claim what's rightfully yours. Think about how proud you feel of someone, even a stranger, when you hear them say "I'm the first one in my family to go to college."

What you claim, especially when true, is powerful.

What is True

Let's end where we began this chapter: You win when what you claim and what people think is in line with what is true. Perception equals your claims times the truth. People will evaluate you based on the extent to which your claims are supported (and amplified) by the truth. Your claims, then, should always begin with a healthy dose of reality. The trouble is, as you'll discover below, that reality can be elusive. The history of the business world is full of stories in which self-deception led them to shoot themselves in the foot. For instance, Volkswagen (VW) Emission Scandal (2015), when it installed software in its diesel vehicles to cheat emissions tests. VW claimed its vehicles were environmentally friendly, but, in reality, they emitted pollutants at levels far above legal limits. Wells Fargo became a notorious financial institution after its 2016 fake account scandal, creating bogus users to meet unrealistic sales targets. How can we forget about Enron? Once considered the most successful energy company. They engaged in self-deception about the true financial health of the company and adopted accounting practices to hide its losses. Consequently, it resulted in one of the most significant global bankruptcies.

Truth is one of the central topics in philosophy. The meaning of truth is something that has been debated for millennia, and although the debates are rarely as cerebral these days as those indulged in by the likes of Aristotle or Aquinas, truth has certainly developed a new salience in this, the age of perceived fake news, alternative facts, and open assault on journalism. Information now rapidly spreads through digital media channels and the line between facts, opinions, and interpretations can sometimes blur. This can lead to situations where businesses and individuals may be more susceptible to misinformation, manipulation, or the distortion of truth.

Several scholarly theories attempt to unpick the truth. One of the most important, from the neo-classical school, is correspondence theory, which holds that what we say and believe is only true if it corresponds to the way things are in reality. In other words, truth exists where our words correspond to the facts. Good start, but what, then, are facts?

According to Northwestern Professor of Philosophy Michael Glanzberg, "facts, for the neo-classical correspondence theory, are entities in their own right. Facts are generally taken to be composed of particulars and properties and relations or universals, at least. The neo-classical correspondence theory thus only makes sense within the setting of a metaphysics that includes such facts."[8]

The basic idea of the correspondence theory is that what we believe or say is true if it corresponds to the way things are – to the facts. The problem with identifying the truth is that, in the process of checking facts and verifying beliefs, you will uncover additional facts and beliefs that also need checking and verifying. In short, the road to truth is never-ending.

If the truth of a matter falls at the very conclusion of our investigation into that claim, then – because inquiries would need to be infinite to reach that conclusion, the truth, as psychiatrist and philosopher Neel Burton explains, "can never be more than our best opinion of that thing."[9] Burton continues that "if best opinion is all that we can hope for, then best opinion is as good as truth, and truth is a redundant concept."[10]

This is a rather fatalist way of looking at things, and there are more helpful and practical ways of understanding the truth. Coherence theory, for example, holds that a belief is true if it satisfactorily coheres with enough other beliefs. Born from the British idealist school, coherence theory rejects the idea of "mind-independent" facts that can stand independent of human perception.

Coherence theory comes with its issues. It infers that people are confined by the four walls of their own beliefs and cannot know anything as real other than the things that make up their particular belief system. Coherence theory also fails to pinpoint what is objectively *true*, instead allowing that there might be many different, incompatible, belief systems.[11]

Some scholars have resolved this tension by suggesting that the most useful, logical, belief systems will prevail – almost like

Darwin's natural selection for truth.[12] Philosophy professor Simon Blackburn notes the replacement of Newtonian mechanics by relativity as an example of this process.[13]

The truth is hard to pinpoint, that is (ironically) one certain thing. Perhaps the best you can do as a business owner, then, is to speak the truth as best you know how. That's not a free pass to make information up. That means a constant reflection on what you're saying and how it aligns with both the corresponding 'facts', as well as the belief system you subscribe to. Lying to others is bad enough, but lying to yourself that you're *not* telling lies? That's no way to live... also extremely confusing.

⊏⊐

Your business story has its core elements, but the way it is perceived is also a major point for your consideration. Those perceptions will come at you in every shape and form, and there's only so much you can do to manage them. What you *do* have control over is what you claim and how it correlates to the truth. What is the truth? Well, you will have to decide for yourself. As Burton puts it:

Truth is constructive and adaptive, while lies are destructive and self-defeating. So how useful is a self-deceptive thought or reaction going to be for you? Are you just covering up an irrational fear, or helping to create a solid foundation for the future? Are you empowering yourself to fulfill your highest potential, or depriving yourself of opportunities for growth and creating further problems down the line? Is the cycle simply going to repeat itself, or will the truth, at last, make you free?[14]

I GUESS that, if you're not a sociopath, you'll feel the truth of your story the first time you tell it. From that point on, it's a matter of never losing the magic.

1. Lumen, "What is perception", *courses.lumenlearning.com*, Accessed: https://courses.lumenlearning.com/waymaker-psychology/chapter/reading-what-is-perception/

2. Ibid.

3. Marshall Segall, Donald Campbell, and Melville Herskovits, "Cultural Differences in the Perception of Geometric Illusions", *Science*, Vol.139, No.3556, pp.769-771.

4. Ibid.

5. Djin Gie Liem, Annemarie Westerbeek, Sascha Wolterink, Frans J. Kok, Cees de Graaf, "Sour Taste Preferences of Children Relate to Preference for Novel and Intense Stimuli", *Chemical Senses*, Vol.29, No.8, 2004, pp.713-720.

6. Stafleu, A., de Graaf, C., van Staveren, W. A., & de Jong, M. A. (1994). Attitudes towards high-fat foods and their low-fat alternatives: Reliability and relationship with fat intake. *Appetite*, Vol.22, No.2, pp.183-196.

7. Jennifer K. South Palomares & Andrew W. Young, "Facial First Impressions of Partner Preference Traits: Trustworthiness, Status, and Attractiveness", *Social Psychological and Personality Science*, Vol.9, No.8, 2018. Pp.990-1000.

8. Michael Glanzberg, "Truth", *Stanford Encyclopedia of Philosophy*, August 16, 2018, Accessed: https://plato.stanford.edu/entries/truth/

9. Neel Burton, "What is Truth: An overview of the philosophy of truth", *psychologytoday.com*, August 23, 2018, Accessed: https://www.psychologytoday.com/nz/blog/hide-and-seek/201808/what-is-truth

10. Ibid.

11. Simon W. Blackburn, "Truth", *Britannica.com*, April 20, 2009, Accessed: https://www.britannica.com/topic/truth-philosophy-and-logic

12. Ibid.

13. Ibid.

14. Neel Burton, "What is Truth: An overview of the philosophy of truth."

CHAPTER 8

FINDING YOUR AUDIENCE

BRINGING Your Story
to **Life**

Finding your audience is almost as important as discovering who you are and identifying your business story. If a tree falls on YouTube and no one clicks to watch it, does it make a sound? In other words, you can have the world's most compelling narrative, but if you aren't telling it to the right crowd, where does that leave you? Discovering and nurturing your story is the yin to your business journey, and finding the platform to tell it is the yang.

When you deliver your story, you want it to make an impact, not fall flat. To achieve that, you need to make sure the time, place, and people are right. Some of the best storytelling in the world is made that way not thanks to the story alone, but thanks to decisions made at the story's periphery: to whom you tell it, where, when, and how.

Colleagues, business partners, potential employees, and

customers all demand a different version of your business story. By properly identifying and segmenting the distinct audiences of your business, you can predict the reception of your story and adjust the content, delivery style, and location to suit.

The Gettysburg Address became associated with Abraham Lincoln not because it was always intended to, but because he took charge of the opportunity to tell a story that the audience of the day was craving. The primary Gettysburg Address was given by Whig Party member Edward Everett, who spoke for a whopping two hours. While Everett's words are rarely recalled, Lincoln's subsequent two-minute oration became one of the most important speeches in history. Lincoln appealed to the sentiment of the occasion, summing up the sacrifices made during the Civil War and striking a tone that, thanks to its blend of emotion and concision, took 271 words. The shelf life far outlives the speaker.

Audience Activation

Find your audience, and your story will take flight. It probably *won't* go down in the history books alongside the Gettysburg Address, but if it's truly meaningful to even one or two people, you've done better than most. We suffer from such incredible information overload in this day and age that much of it is digested passively, disinterestedly, or not at all. Your aim in telling your story should be to take a passive audience and transform them into a captive one.

Every consumable source of information – be that magazines, posters, music, films, games, and speeches – has an audience, and they all fall into the passive or captive category.

Captive audiences are those who have the potential to interact with you – who are in the same theater, board room, or audition hall as you, and who can not only hear your story but see you perform it. When visiting a grocery store, you may encounter staff offering free product samples. Shoppers become captive audiences as they try the samples and listen to the product pitch.

Passive audiences, on the other hand, are the scrollers. They're generally the audience you'll find on Twitter or Instagram. They're reading and consuming, but when the microwave dings or their show comes on the TV – you've lost them. That's not to say that passive audiences are less valuable than captive ones. They're simply different, and you should choose with care which version of your story suits which type of audience.

Passive audiences are affected by information. They receive data and experience it at a sensory level – they hear what you're saying, see how you're presenting the information, and ingest it. Captive audiences are more active. They feel involved in what you are telling them, and because of this are more likely to retain the information and remember it later. Rather than simply ingesting what you tell them, captive audiences process and perceive the information – interacting with the information to create meaning and make a connection with your story.

You can transform your passive audiences into captive ones, but it is crucial to recognize the importance of content to each generation. Each generation embraces a changing balance of values, preferences, technology adoption levels, and communication channels. Imagine we aim to advertise our toothpaste brand (toothpaste is a generational commonality). What kind of content will appeal to each generation? What should we consider? Baby Boomers would respond better to the traditional media, highlight the quality, freshness, and dentist-recommended aspects of the toothpaste. Nostalgia can be a powerful tool to engage them, such as a campaign titled "Unforgettable Smile: A Journey Through the Decades with

Our Toothpaste." However, Gen X appreciates a balanced approach (both online and offline means). Creating content that emphasizes the importance of dental health and how modern technology plays a role, such as "Advanced Dental Care for the Modern Age" will likely have a greater effect.

As for me? I'm a millennial. A term loved by those who coined it and generally disliked by those of us labeled by it. Millennials were the first generation with a label created by marketers to identify who we are. We were the generation at the dawn of big data and data mining for advertising. I distinctly remember sitting in agency meetings and hearing about "what millennials think" or what we're doing. It was as though connecting with us would unlock all the profit in the world. To be fair, that's what attracted clients to our agency to begin with. Banyan Branch (the place I worked that would later be acquired by Deloitte), was a social media agency staffed with about 40 people all under 30 years old. My job was to manage the social media pages and social media for, among other brands, FOX's biggest shows like the Simpsons, Bob's Burgers (from its first episode), and 24. We didn't know it at the time, but our generation had unique values that were born out of 9/11, climate change, information access, and the 2008 financial crash that would shape how we moved through the world. To put it short, we cared.

Back to our ad... Millennials value digital content and support social causes so highlighting sustainable packaging, cruelty-free ingredients, or social impact initiatives, such as "Eco-Friendly Toothpaste: Smile for a Cause" is the best option. Gen Z on the other hand, as digital natives, prefer short-form video content and interactive campaigns. Promote creative challenges or user-generated content on platforms like TikTok to engage them, such as a song that invites users to create an edit to with the label of #brushitoff. Get your audience involved. Look for tactics that can help bridge the gap between the passive and captive audience for a business.

- *Improve your social media content:* Narrate compelling brand stories, use attention grabbing visuals and mix up content formats. Ensure the underlying message is highly relevant.
- *Audience segmentation:* Research the pain points of the audience and use algorithms to suggest products/services based on their needs. Avoid bombarding them with ads they have nothing to do with.
- *Develop an emotional connection:* Be authentic and relatable
- *Interactivity:* Incorporate pools, surveys, encourage user generated content like reviews, comments, feedbacks.
- *Community Building:* Foster a sense of community among your audience, where they can connect, share, and collaborate. Host forums, discussion boards, or social media groups where like-minded individuals can interact.

The type of audience you find yourself facing will depend on many factors - firstly, on who you have chosen to be your audience. Are you talking to Instagram followers? A boardroom of investors? Customers via a press release? Secondly, the nature of your audience depends on the people in that group themselves. Are they a strong collective or a group of disparate individuals? Are they highly motivated to interact, or is it in their best interests to passively receive the information?

It will come as no surprise that the most valuable audiences for your business are captive, active ones. How then, to turn passive listeners into captive ones?

Be the Fed-Ex Guy

Found your audience? (Dad joke incoming...) Now it's time to *deliver*. I don't mean that as a verb either. I mean it as an imperative. Get out there and perform your story. Don't underestimate the importance of developing an audience plan in parallel to your story blueprint. You're an entrepreneur and focused on the business side of things, but if you were a multinational company (or any company for that matter), you'd have a communications team, a marketing advisor, and an audience segmentation strategy. You might not have those people now, so it's on you to fill the gap.

You're not going to be telling your whole story and nothing but your story so help you God every time you step up to a podium. That means that every time you speak to a new audience, you'll want to reflect on who they are, what they want from you, what you want from them, where you are, and what they've heard before. Adapt to the situation, otherwise, you'll lose that magical authenticity. Never lose the magic!

- Write it down first.

You might be the ultimate wingman, but very, *very* few people are good at winging a speech. That doesn't mean you can't ad-lib, go with your gut, change tack, or sound unrehearsed, it just means write it down first. Even just a few bullet points will help. Once you have them, take a step back and ask yourself:

1. Is this the story I should be giving to *this* particular audience?
2. Am I forgetting any key points?
3. Am I telling the story in a logical order?

Feel free to deliver it off the cuff, but the act of writing it down first allows you to assess whether you'll be hitting the right mark with your audience of the day. For the record, I advise the same for giving a wedding speech. Write it down first, make notes, and by then you probably won't need anything beyond a notecard.

- Practice, practice, practice

There's a strange thing about speechmaking. Often when we're afraid of it, we put next to no effort in. It's as if we're scared of falling too far, so we make sure the drop between effort and failure is minimal. The fact is, though, that a little effort beforehand almost *guarantees* a better outcome. Any presentation, interview, introduction, or oration should have a full run-through at least once before showtime.

- Delivery

You can take entire courses on presentation delivery so I'm not going to teach you how to suck eggs. Suffice to say, there are a million and one things you can do to make your story 'pop' while you're telling it ... and you should do those things. From standing up straight to maintaining eye contact with your audience to speaking at a natural, conversational pace – if you practice and execute these tactics, your delivery will be all the better for it.

You may be a natural. You can capture a room and naturally

command a group. What makes you this way, and can these skills be learned by others without this natural talent? That all depends on how much you can overcome your fears and reservations and make the effort that your story deserves. If you're passionate enough about your business and its back story, then hopefully that takes the edge off any lack of performance gene.

Love or hate social media, some of the best business communicators can be found among the social media elite. Sheryl Sandberg, Facebook COO, is an excellent example of an entrepreneur who gets her audience. Adept at turning tech talk into consumable, engaging information for all, Sandberg has a commanding, but light, speaking style that audiences find engaging. A major proponent of storytelling in business, she argues that "...stories are vital." They're how we explain our past and they are how we set expectations for our future. And they help us build the common understanding that creates a community in the first place."[1]

Sandberg first began telling stories in her professional life when, in 2010, she was due to give a TED talk about women in the workplace. Armed with screeds of statistics, a friend encouraged her just before the conference began to weave more personal stories into her presentation. She took the advice, telling the audience that when departing from her home in San Francisco, she'd had to cope with leaving her 3-year-old daughter behind despite her heart-wrenching pleas of "Mommy, don't go!" The speech was a resounding success, and went viral, leading to Sandberg's best-selling book *Lean In* on the same topic.

Despite this success, Sandberg took time to fully embrace her new storytelling approach. When writing *Lean In*, Sandberg has described how the drafts contained more statistics than stories:

I wrote the first chapter; I thought it was fabulous. It was chock-full of data and figures. I had three pages on matrilineal Maasai tribes and their sociological patterns. My husband read it, and he was like, this is like eating your Wheaties. No one--and I apologize to Wheaties--no one, no one will read this book. And I realized through the process that I had to be more honest and more open, and I had to tell my stories.[2]

Elsewhere in social media land, Twitter and Square co-founder Jack Dorsey (love him or hate him) is another great example of a businessman who knows how to deliver. Even his business baby, Twitter, is all about effective delivery – a platform on which billions of users from around the world can interact quickly and concisely about endless complex topics. It's not just Dorsey's product that wins in the storytelling stakes, though. He also has a great personal command of stories and analogies.

Dorsey makes a point of drawing ideas from around his companies, allowing all his employees every week to ask questions, make suggestions, and feel connected to him and the heart of the business. By making time to ensure a captive audience among his staff, he also allows himself to be captivated by his staff - a significant improvement from a company intranet with an "Ask the CEO" function. If you take the time to understand your different audiences, you'll realize just how much employees like FaceTime with their leaders.

Like Sandberg, Dorsey is a master at using stories to connect with his audiences. He comes across as genuine and approachable, knows how to use movements, gestures, and visuals to best effect, and believes in simplifying complexity – something audiences always appreciate.

Your Story is an Experience. How You Tell it Should be Too.

You've experienced your own story. You lived the highs and the lows. You had a tough childhood, swooned through some heady romances, dreamed some kick-ass dreams, and fist-pumped the air when your first sale came through. You've experienced your story, and how you tell it should be an experience for those who hear it. Don't be that drunk uncle who stands around at his niece's wedding holding fort with the microphone and forcing everyone in attendance to charge their glasses and settle in for the long haul. You're a human being, not a drone or a Lieutenant-General leading the Charge of the Light Brigade.

Here's how to avoid derailing your great story with bad delivery.

- Wrong place, wrong time

If you don't tailor your story and its delivery, then you're missing a major trick in the storytelling game. Is English the first language of your audience? You might want to slow down your delivery if not. Even if it's an audience of two, they want to feel that you are speaking to them and a lack of awareness is likely to fall flat. Remember Juicero? A startup to revolutionize the juicing industry by creating a high-tech juicer but it failed to align its story with the audience. Instead of addressing the practical needs and desires of their target audience they focus on the tech part only, resulting in a lack of market acceptance and, eventually, the company's demise.

- Stuck to the stump

A stump speech is useful to have in your back pocket – that narrative you can trot out again and again to a wide range of audiences. Some entrepreneurs, however, get stuck on the stump. They're practically superglued to it. If you're rolling out the same yarn over and over, and the same people are in your audience, they're going to get bored of you and your story. It's certainly extra work, but you need to be agile and mix things up. For instance, Disney's narrative is built around the themes of magic, imagination, and storytelling. From its earliest days with iconic characters like Mickey Mouse to its contemporary successes with franchises like Marvel, Star Wars, and Pixar, Disney has consistently emphasized the power of storytelling to inspire and entertain. But why don't people get bored? Though they have the same narrative, they use technology and a variety of platforms to reinvent the same stories they've been telling for decades.

Don't get stuck.

• Nail the narrative

People remember stories. It's as simple as that. Details, data and pensive thoughts are all well and good but don't expect your audience to walk away with any of that information. What they'll remember are stories. Good ones. Good stories use CROW to hit all the right points. Head back to Chapters Two and Three if you need a refresher on just how to nail the art of narrative. How can one forget Mr. Chouinard, the founder of Patagonia, when he decided to transfer the ownership of $3 billion of company worth to a specially designed trust and an NGO. It's not just a business move, but a compelling narrative that will leave a lasting impact over generations and earn the admiration of aspiring entrepreneurs. It's a story of a founder who values his company's mission and foundational principles above all else. Haters will say it's a PR move and that actually protects his assets from tax. If so, all the more power of using story to make a moment worth headlines. Great stories like this one are memorable because they inspire and resonate with people on a deeper level, transcending business transactions and becoming part of a company's identity.

- Stop selling

No matter how much you need something from your audience, never let them feel that. This is an unspoken social contract between the audience and the storyteller. The audience may even know they're there to be sold to, but if it's even a tiny bit explicit you'll turn them off. Be humble. Be grateful. Talk about things that matter. Then, and only then, talk up your company. Straight selling is empty words to audiences. Stories that explain, in a genuine way, with an engaging narrative, why your product helps people. Those are stories that will help your business flourish.

I've been sold to countless times, but there's one story that really stuck with me. I was visiting my dermatologist's office for a routine skin check (something I'll assume you do regally as well...). Everything seemed fine until the end of the appointment when the doctor said, "Our receptionist will give you some great sunscreen, and I'll make sure they take care of you."

For a moment, it felt like genuine concern for my health. But when I went to pay, I noticed a sneaky $45 charge for that sunscreen which left me uneasy and questioning their intentions. Not only did the lose my trust, they lost my business.

⸻

Comfort is key to a good life and an even better delivery. If you're not comfortable, both in your skin and in the way you communicate, you're going to face an uphill battle. If you find yourself lacking comfort in these areas, it's okay to make adjustments and see how you can flip the script. The more comfortable you are, the more comfortable your audience is. Making an audience uncomfortable has an equal and opposite effect.

Plenty of entrepreneurs' storytelling falls on this sword. Mark Pincus, CEO and Founder of social game developer Zynga, is one of the most successful entrepreneurs but certainly had to mature in the way he communicates. Early on, Pincus's visual and verbal cues undermined his message, and, as a result, his achievements and story are overshadowed by a condescending arrogance. Pincus also overdoes the jargon and fails to tell his stories in a logical, digestible narrative – making them difficult to follow and lacking in impact.

Olympic swimmer Ryan Lochte is another example of how likability can have a major impact on a personal brand. Lochte is undoubtedly a talented athlete with great accomplishments in his career, but his manner of speaking – parodied by Seth McFarlane and Seth Myers on SNL - leaves audiences flat. Not only does it come across as indifferent and a little blockish, but his habit of dropping keywords from sentences also throws listeners off. Again, there's no taking away from Lochte's skill as a swimmer – but as a communicator? Lochte loses people, and it's to the detriment of his brand. His aloof behavior has cost him sponsorship dollars and hindered his ability to remain elite.

Making it Personal

How often do you watch a speaker – let's say a TED Talk presenter – and know that deep down the topic is super interesting, but the speaker just doesn't seem ready? They're looking down at the teleprompter, they're reading, but their delivery lacks the ups and downs of regular speech. When that happens to an audience, you lose them. Even if they're still interested in what you're saying, their brain will be deep in a running commentary, critiquing your stance, tone, eye contact – everything. In the middle of watching the talk, your mind wanders and you start multitasking. This is not a captive audience. This is the difference between a TED talk and a TEDxPodunk talk. As I'm writing this, a TED Talk episode from 2012 with Daphne Koller (co-founder of Coursera) titled "What We're Learning from Online Education" just crossed my mind. Despite an important and interesting topic, Koller's delivery came across as somewhat disconnected and technical to me. She heavily relied on slides and data, which made her talk feel more like a lecture than a TED Talk. While the content was valuable, her presentation style didn't fully capture the audience's attention or convey the excitement and potential of online education as effectively as it could have. This reminds us of the importance of a balance between a compelling topic and delivering it in a way that resonates deeply with the audience.

When somebody tells a story like this, it makes you wonder: am I listening to your story? Or am I hearing the story you've scripted for yourself? It's the same story when a best man gets up at a wedding, fumbles with his notes, and carefully reads his crafted speech. This is your best friend. You can honor your friendship better than that. Be genuine. Look at the audience and tell them how much he means to you. This doesn't mean you can't prepare beforehand – you should – it just means you should try hard not to look like you're trying ... too hard. A tough tightrope to walk. I believe in you.

Performing doesn't come naturally to us all. Sometimes it feels disingenuous to even put dedicated effort into telling a good story. But just remember, putting the effort in doesn't change the truth of your narrative. We live in an age in which the performance of who we are and the persona of what we're becoming is just as important as the truth.

---

1. Sheryl Sandberg, quoted in "Sheryl Sandberg Reflects on Her Husband's Death and How She Bounced Back", *entrepreneur.com*, Accessed: https://www.entrepreneur.com/article/294224

2. Sheryl Sandberg, quoted in Carmine Gallo "Dave Goldberg's Feedback Helped Make 'Lean In' a Must Read," *forbes.com*, May 5, 2015, Accessed: https://www.forbes.com/sites/carminegallo/2015/05/05/dave-goldbergs-feedback-helped-make-lean-in-a-must-read/#720216d35918

CHAPTER 9

IMPOSTOR SYNDROME

YOU THINK You're Not Worthy
but You're Wrong

Few things evoke the entrepreneurial spirit quite as successfully as a rags-to-riches tale. Packed full of that heady mix of despondency, hope, moral fortitude, and inevitable wads of cash, these stories appeal to our intrinsic desire to rise and conquer. Full-time optimist Tony Robbins suffered through an abusive childhood, ran away from home, worked as a janitor, and never went to college. Now? Multi-millionaire. FUBU founder Daymond John grew up in Queens, waited tables at Red Lobster, then sold his handmade hats on a street corner. These days? Multi-millionaire. J.K. Rowling wrote Harry Potter over a cold cup of coffee while being a single mother on welfare. Fast forward twenty-five years. *Billionaire*. We love to hear of people just like us who have broken free from the mundane, the everyday, and who have really captured success.

These are all inspirational tales. But what if you're just ...

normal? What if you're doing okay? You have money left in the bank after paying your bills. You have two loving parents. You didn't grow up in a war zone. You're not a struggling single parent. You had a good education. Can you still have a great business story?

In this chapter, I want to dispel the myth that you need a rags-to-riches tale to tell people how you got where you are today. Relating to this, we'll look at one of the biggest challenges entrepreneurs face in projecting their business story to the world: impostor syndrome.

Impostor syndrome is the little devil on your shoulder telling you "you're not successful enough, you're not smart enough, you're not worthy of 'making it' in business, and you don't deserve much of this." Often impostor syndrome manifests in the feeling that "I'm not the right person to live this life," or "my story isn't compelling enough to make me a success." It can affect entrepreneurs at any stage of their journey, from startup founders to seasoned business owners. One notable example of an entrepreneur who openly discussed struggling with imposter syndrome is Sheryl Sandberg, the Chief Operating Officer (COO) of Facebook. Despite her impressive career, she has experienced imposter syndrome and felt like a fraud at times, even when holding high-profile positions. Sandberg's openness about her own imposter syndrome has resonated with many aspiring entrepreneurs and professionals. Bear in mind, it's not something every business owner will encounter, but it's certainly a very common shared experience.

I promise you this, there will be times that you feel like you don't know what you're doing even when you know exactly what you are doing.

"I don't know that it's possible to be entirely rid of impostor syndrome but I do manage it better today. What has helped me is

learning to recognize it so I can deal with my feelings rationally and talk myself down."

MIKAELA KINER, REVERB CEO

Impostor syndrome can be, at its worst, incredibly debilitating, and at best, a massive energy suck and time waster. To get over this hurdle, you'll need to stare the issue in the eye, understand it, and rob it of its hold over you. We'll do that here, but first, let's take a look at just why the rags-to-riches trope has endured so relentlessly in the entrepreneur's consciousness, and what you can do if you don't happen to have one of your own.

A Tradition of Triumph

Why is it that we're so drawn to the success story of the underdog? There are many things – from psychological to cultural – that cause this predilection, just like we're inclined at any given time in history to be more attracted to bigger or smaller female forms, bearded or clean-shaven men, Coca-Cola or Pepsi ... the list goes on.

From a cultural perspective, rags-to-riches tales solidified their place in the American subconscious during the 19th century. Part of the "American dream," the ability of poor, uneducated people to rise up the ranks and make their fortunes appealed to the pioneering spirit of those who chose to settle in the Americas. The hero of the tale typically hailed from a rural or foreign background, and then, as American history researcher Eyal Naveh explains: "thanks to sheer effort, hard work, and virtuous behavior reached success – usually defined in material terms."[1]

This narrative theme became folkloric – a dream sold mostly to young men from poor rural or immigrant backgrounds to instill in them the benefits of hard work and a sound moral compass. In his 1991 article "The Transformation of the 'Rags to Riches' Stories: Business Biographies of Success in the Progressive Era and the 1920s," Naveh explains that the rural land "represented all that was moral, virtuous and vital to many Americans. Rural life required hard work, but according to popular belief it built a sound, democratic, and independent character, typical of the American experience in the New World."[2]

The rise of the successful businessman born of a rural, uneducated background gradually became, in Naveh's words, a "common cultural discourse" aimed at giving "meaning to the American experience."[3] It became so accepted that businessmen even began to base their legitimacy on that meteoric rise. As Naveh notes: "The nineteenth century 'rags to riches' stories stressed informal and practical learning rather than formal education as the best preparation for success. Some businessmen were happy to note that they had acquired only elementary education and had not finished high school."[4]

So nurtured was this narrative that it became an entrenched part of the national psyche, even influencing the literary favorites of the age. During the last two decades of the 19th century, author Horatio Alger penned dozens of young adult novels which captured the spirit of the rags-to-riches tale. Perhaps best known was his *Ragged Dick* (no comment), which followed the fortunes of a shoeshine boy who wished to turn over a new leaf and "grow up 'spectable".[5] Alger's books were in no way masterpieces, but found enormous popularity because they mirrored and nurtured the sentiment of the era - one of the golden ages of the American self-made man – that with the right attitude and hard work, one could dream big and chart a course to success.

. . .

"I've learned that the more I share my own vulnerabilities, the more people feel comfortable sharing theirs. And that's when we can really connect and make a difference."

-TINA SHARKEY, BRANDLESS CEO

Wired For It

A penchant for poverty-to-penthouse narratives isn't just a cultural hand-me-down, we're also psychologically inclined to enjoy stories in which the underdog works hard and makes it to the top. Why? According to a study by Dylan Wiward, our brains like to know that our motivation is worthwhile, and that what we do has an impact on our lives. In Wiwad's words, "perceiving high income mobility may satisfy certain psychological needs as per the theory of Motivated Social Cognition, and these needs may be crucial to emotional well-being as described by Self-Determination Theory."[6]

According to Self-determination theory, the principal prerequisites for emotional well-being are autonomy, competency, and relatedness. Similarly, Motivated Social Cognition theory holds that individuals will often adopt beliefs so as to fulfill strong psychological needs. Wiwad hypothesizes that "Under the umbrella of MSC, it is plausible that the belief that one has high income mobility satisfies myriad psychological motivations, such as the motivation to maintain a high level of emotional well-being. Belief in high income mobility may also satisfy psychological needs for autonomy and competence which, as SDT researchers point out, are crucial to emotional well-being."[7]

By pursuing rags-to-riches tales, then, we're seeking to confirm to our agitated brains that our motivation and hard work is all worthwhile, and that our tendency toward autonomy and competency will pay off. This helps to explain why the "hero's journey" remains one of the most popular and persistent templates for fiction – from novels to the silver screen – involving a central 'hero' character who embarks on a journey, has a crisis, wins and triumphs, and then returns to his regular life a changed man. We are psychologically inclined to feel a pull to these types of tales, because they speak to our innate human desire to prevail, learn, and grow. As Phil Cousineau puts it:

> *The journey of the hero is about the courage to seek the depths; the image of creative rebirth; the eternal cycle of change within us; the uncanny discovery that the seeker is the mystery which the seeker seeks to know. The hero journey is a symbol that binds, in the original sense of the word, two distant ideas, the spiritual quest of the ancients with the modern search for identity....*[8]

Communication coach Carmine Gallo gives another great explanation of just why we're so drawn to this rags-to-riches, hero's journey narrative:

Struggle makes your life story more interesting for others to hear because the best things in nature are products of struggle. Pearls, diamonds, and award-winning wine represent nature's conquest over adversity. For example, the best wine grapes come from steep slopes or rocky soil that stresses the roots and creates fruit bursting with flavor. Winemakers say grapes that grow in harsh soil have more "character." We like stories with a diamond at the end, a satisfying resolution to the struggle. Inspiring leaders often speak in the story of adversity to create an emotional bond with their audiences. If you've been through rocky times, it's important to embrace your back story and to share it with others. The experience has formed your character and makes you an interesting person. Don't feel as though you have to expose all the skeletons in the closet to connect with your audiences, but a story of triumph over adversity is irresistible for a reason. We're wired for it.[9]

It may naturally appeal to our brains, but the rags-to-riches narrative theme has come under fire from a number of essayists, activists, and social reformers, who argue that despite the prevalence of these stories, in reality it is only a small number of people who climb the social and financial ladder from the very bottom right to the top. Manuel Peña, for example, argues that:

... in putting the onus for failure on the individual, and not on external circumstances such as class inequality, any potential criticism of the economic system or its class structure is effectively nullified. But this is where the most insidious aspect of the rags-to-riches narrative takes effect. In assigning blame to the individual for personal failure, the myth absolves those who control the levers of economic power and its exploitative practices by displacing the reality of class (and race and gender) inequality onto a false signifier – the "morally defective" individual.[10]

Wiwad's study ultimately agrees, finding that "While the present results indicate that a belief in high income mobility leads to higher emotional well-being in the short term, it is possible that the nature of this relationship changes over time. Being told that income mobility is high may lead to a momentary affect boost as people imagine positive changes, but these hedonic outcomes may sour when people fail to see a positive change in their own economic situation."[11]

Uninspiring Origins

In his aptly-titled book *Pour Your Heart Into It,* Howard Schultz – former CEO and now executive chairman of Starbucks – claims that "the more uninspiring your origins, the more likely you are to use your imagination and invent worlds where everything seems possible."

I'll let you decide if you think that's true or not. What's certain is that the right to tell a compelling business story and to grow a powerful business does not reside solely with those born into poverty, immigrants, members of minority groups, or people who have survived a terminal illness. You may read these rags-to-riches tales and consider yourself decidedly vanilla, but that's an unhelpful comparison that will take you nowhere. If you didn't have a major struggle to get where you are today, consider yourself blessed, not hindered. Yes, a little adversity can breed incredible success in the entrepreneurial world, but it's not a prerequisite.

According to a 2019 study of small business trends by Guidant Financial, 33% of entrepreneurs have only a high school diploma.[12] That means more than 60% went to college. Four percent even have a doctorate.[13] What does this prove? You don't have to go to college to become a businessperson, and you also don't need a high school drop-out story to give yourself the rags-to-riches chops. Entrepreneurs are a mixed bag, and with that mix comes a full rainbow of fascinating tales. Don't try and fit into the rags-to-riches mold if that's not you.

A prime example of a vanilla business background that still makes for a compelling story is that king of the entrepreneurs, Bill Gates. Gates did not grow up in the favelas of Rio. He came from a relatively affluent family, attended a private preparatory school, and studied at Harvard University. His story, then, is not in his rise from the mean streets of Seattle to the wealthiest man on the planet. His story is in his intellect, his talent, his innovation, and his savvy.

Gates showed an interest in programming from an early age and wrote his first software program in the eighth grade. He was also recruited by his school to write their student information system software, which was used to schedule students into their different classes. Sensing an opportunity, Gates altered the code so that it placed him in classes with – in his words – "a disproportionate number of interesting girls."[14] This is Bill Gates' story. There is no element of "rags" in it, but there are certainly riches!

Experience builds character and character adds value, yes. Do not be under the illusion, though, that this experience needs to be soul-destroying, back-breaking, or any other kind of painful experience. What matters more than the experience itself is how you turned it into a lesson, and how you communicate that lesson to your audience.

Impostor Syndrome

The more we succumb to the idea that a good business story needs to have a wow factor, the more debilitated we can become by our own "middle-of-the-road" experience. Not only that, but despite hard work, education, and experience, entrepreneurs often find themselves feeling fraudulent, under-qualified, inexperienced, and unworthy. These feelings are classic symptoms of "impostor syndrome," and while they affect people from all walks of life and a wide range of professions, entrepreneurs are particularly vulnerable as innovators and ideas-people are thrown into the world of hustling.

Entrepreneur and author Kyle Eschenroeder acknowledges the susceptibility of entrepreneurs to impostor syndrome in a 2018 blog post, explaining that: "We're in this weird culture where you've got to sell yourself aggressively while remaining "authentic." You think you need to be perfect but you also need to feel free to fail. You need to be yourself and more! It's all set up to make you feel like a fraud."[15]

So what exactly is impostor syndrome? First of all, it's not really a "syndrome" but a set of beliefs that undermine your self-belief. The term "impostor phenomenon" was first coined in the 1978 paper "The Impostor Phenomenon in High Achieving Women: Dynamics and Therapeutic Intervention" written by clinical psychologists Pauline Clance and Suzanne Imes.[16] The psychologists later explained that they preferred the term "impostor experience," because "condition" or "syndrome" suggests a mental illness, and the impostor experience is much more common to the human experience.

Clance and Imes identified three key "symptoms" of impostor syndrome – and individuals suffering from the experience may suffer from one or all. These are, as psychologist Dr. Sandi Mann summarizes:

1. The belief that others have an inflated view of your abilities or skills.
2. The fear that you will be found out or exposed as a fake.
3. The persistent attribution of success to external factors, such as luck or an extraordinary level of hard work.[17]

The *causes* of impostor syndrome, Mann explains, are varied. It's an affliction high-achievers in particular can suffer from, and it affects men and women equally. Mann identifies three triggers that are particularly likely to cause impostor feelings:

- When first 'qualifying' in your field.
- When starting a new course.

• Receiving a promotion at work.

When it comes to business owners and entrepreneurs, there are numerous reasons to consider. For instance, high expectations; entrepreneurs often set high expectations for themselves and their businesses, aspiring to achieve remarkable success. A startup founder might expect rapid growth and market dominance within a year, and if this doesn't happen, they may feel like they're not living up to their own standards. Then comes comparisons; entrepreneurs often compare their progress and success against that of their more established peers, industry leaders, or even competitors. This constant comparison can lead to feelings of inadequacy, self-doubt, and ultimately Impostor Syndrome. Consider the budding entrepreneurs who have launched a small e-commerce store. They might find themselves comparing their store's growth, revenue, and customer base to that of a well-established, multinational corporation. When they perceive their business as falling short in these comparisons, they may start questioning their own capabilities and qualifications, despite the vast differences in resources and experience between the two entities. Third is negative feedback; negative feedback, whether from customers, investors, or peers, can reinforce impostor feelings. Last but not least is perfectionism: entrepreneurs often strive for perfection in their work, setting unattainable standards for themselves.

You know who is experiencing imposter syndrome right now? Me. The nerves that course through my stomach now are the same ones that did so when I gave this lecture the first time. And the second time. And the year after. And the time I recently gave it as a keynote for the American Advertising Federation. If there's one thing I don't like about telling my story, it's that doing so almost makes it feel less authentic. The belief that I've become who I am because of who I've been is always going to be scrutinized. Looking back at Dr. Mann's criteria, I feel the need to prove my abilities and skills even though I know that's virtually impossible with people new to my life. Not only would that take tremendous effort, but also a tremendous amount of ego and value signaling, which just aren't a part of my personality. The fear of being exposed isn't constant but pops up depending on the people in the room. Sitting at the table with people who I've admired, researched, or worked with often imbues that feeling of "I don't belong here."

As a producer, there are parts of the job, even certain industry terms, that I won't know. At that moment, I feel like a fake even though I've been doing the job for 15 years. My insecurities stem from not being a film school student and having a complete street education for the job I've had for most of my professional life. Even when people ask me for camera advice, I feel like an imposter because I don't have the best answer ready to go. In reality, that's not even something I would know, but it is a production tool so... shouldn't I know? That third part of the criteria is almost a full part of my body: attribution to luck or hard work. Truthfully, I do believe that a lot of life is a combination of dumb luck and doing the work to be ready for it. That might be a part of my imposter syndrome, but I surely won't be shaking it anytime soon. Just because I know it to be true, doesn't mean I have the power (or desire) to change. Imposter syndrome, at least in part, motivates me to prepare more than the average person.

"The first step in overcoming imposter syndrome is recognizing that it's a real thing. It's not just you. It's not just in your head. It's a real thing."

-ARIANNA HUFFINGTON, THRIVE GLOBAL CEO

Slaying the Dragon

Do you think you're an impostor? Chances are, you're probably not. If you truly are an imposter and a con artist, this is not the book you should be reading! In order to move forward and conquer, there's a psychological barrier to owning your success.

Activist and writer Maya Angelou once admitted: "I have written eleven books, but each time I think, 'uh oh, they're going to find out now. I've run a game on everybody, and they're going to find me out." I have thought this same thought more than one time writing this, my second book. Michelle Pfeiffer has similar fears: "I still think people will find out that I'm really not very talented. I'm really not very good. It's all been a big sham." And Kate Winslet feels the same: "Sometimes I wake up in the morning before going off to a shoot, and I think, I can't do this. I'm a fraud."

Impostor syndrome is a complex beast – and often the result of many intertwined insecurities, personality traits, and even genetics. The good news is that you can, and should, slay this dragon. Taking away this feeling will not make you less humble. It will make you more confident in yourself, more efficient, and more successful. Try one or all of these tips and see if you feel more confident in putting yourself out there:

- Stop comparing.

We live in the Age of Comparison. Whereas our great-grandparents had a handful of folk from around town to gossip about and compare themselves to, we can follow any of the ONE BILLION active monthly Instagram users. The world of comparing, critiquing, and subsequent self-flagellation is now our oyster. Of course this does no good to anybody's self-confidence. It's no coincidence that this Age of Comparison is also our Age of Anxiety. Anxiety disorders literally affect more than 18% of the population[18] as of last year.

You are different compared to everybody else that you know. You are less attractive than many (no offense), and less smart than a great number (also no offense), and will probably never be as wealthy as that elite few (I'm making a point, hang tight). You are different. This means that you have something different, something unique, to offer — your perspective, your savvy, your experience, your product. We now live in a niche world. Feeling like an impostor is a waste of time because, if you are you, there's no chance for fraud!

- Kick perfection where it hurts.

Perfect is the enemy of done. That's the only thing I'm going to underline in this book for you (as we all nod in appreciation for Voltaire). If you have perfectionist tendencies, you'll understand what I'm talking about here. Sometimes we are so consumed by the idea of needing to be 'the best' that we are consumed by inertia – rendered unable to think or act effectively. When we hold ourselves to this impossible standard, anything we do attempt inevitably falls short of our expectations. We go about our days believing we are 'sub-par' and leave ourselves wide open to a visit from the impostor syndrome elf.

If you're a lawyer, for example, you're faced with knowing and understanding a vast legal system and its literature. That's tough, and sometimes you'll feel overwhelmed and underprepared. You'll compare yourself to Amal Clooney, and then feel like crap because you're not an internationally renowned human rights lawyer draped in Oscar de la Renta with George Clooney flanking your left. Luckily, Amal isn't perfect either. Acknowledge that your perception of her characteristics and your perception of your own flaws are out of whack.

- Accept that you are an impostor and get good at it.

If doing away with comparisons and perfectionism doesn't work, there's one thing left to try. Embrace your feelings of impostor syndrome and live up to the 'act' you feel you are making. In other terms, "fake it until you make it." Do this long enough and you'll realize that you were running on your own merits all along.

This doesn't mean you should lie, make up facts, or deceive others. As Kyle Eschenroeder explains:

We are often put in the position of "expert". When this happens people look at you like you should know *everything* about a topic. We can't know everything about anything though. If I'm in a situation where there is potential to *actually* be a fraud—ie bullsh*t about things I don't know—I just say what I can instead. People respect this much more. Admit that you don't yet have the answer but you'll find it. Admit that you haven't found the perfect solution but you've come close enough.[19]

Don't Tell Tales

I have a secret. We almost all grew up poor, at least statistically speaking. We all had to struggle. We've all felt alone. You have faced challenges in your life, and these remain your story – regardless of whether you'd win in a game of "whose childhood was worse." Don't be inauthentic. Don't make up a sob story for the sake of winning support or building a rags-to-riches narrative. Take what you do have and tell it honestly.

Your struggle doesn't need to be your childhood or your personal circumstances. You can tell the challenge of product development or the issue that led you to invent the thing you invented. Bill Gates was raised in a stable family. His early education afforded him the opportunity to learn computers, but his professional dedication may have been, in part, fueled by the loss of his grade school best friend in a climbing accident. His story is in his hard work, vulnerability, and commitment. The question now is, where's yours?

<hr>

1. Eyal Naveh, "The Transformation of the "Rags to Riches" Stories: Business Biographies of Success in the Progressive Era and the 1920s," *American Studies International*, Vol.29, No.1, 1991, p.60
2. Ibid, pg 66
3. Ibid, pg 61
4. Ibid, pg 67
5. Horatio Alger, *Ragged Dick*, (Levelland: Laughing Dog Press, 2019), p.46
6. Dylan Wiwad, "The Rags-to-Riches Story of Income Mobility and Its Impact on Emotional Wellbeing", *Master's Thesis*, (Simon Fraser University, 2015), Accessed: https://thesiscommons.org/5wf4a/?fbclid=IwAR3BKhdQqxjjDgOMMkqhYlmK4oPDBaEL4zoxK_6rjdAunDq9_Bi_7KFzaOM
7. Ibid.
8. Phil Cousineau (ed), *The Hero's Journey: Joseph Campbell on his Life and Work*, (Novato: Joseph Campbell Foundation, 2003), p.xix
9. Carmine Gallo, "Why We're Wired to Love Rags-to-Riches Stories", *inc.com*, April 21, 2017, Accessed: https://www.carminegallo.com/wired-love-rags-riches-stories/?fbclid=IwARoLtDHojEBPqs2sL9StlTkSGAuE64-A5XzFUTsCBZtFRFeW6Gd6OJMA2vw
10. Manuel Peña, *American Mythologies: Semiological Sketches*, (Oxon, Routledge, 2016), p.71

11. Dylan Wiwad, "The Rags-to-Riches Story of Income Mobility and Its Impact on Emotional Wellbeing."

12. Guidant Financial, "Current Small Business Trends and Statistics," *guidantfinancial.com*, 2019, Accessed: https://www.guidantfinancial.com/small-business-trends/

13. Ibid.

14. Bill Gates, "Remarks by Bill Gates, co-chair," *gatesfoundation.org*, September 23, 2005, Accessed: https://www.gatesfoundation.org/media-center/speeches/2005/09/bill-gates-lakeside-school

15. Kyle Eschenroeder, "21 Proven Ways to Overcome Impostor Syndrome", *startbros.com*, 2018, Accessed: https://startupbros.com/21-ways-overcome-impostor-syndrome/

16. Pauline Clance & Suzanne Imes, "The Impostor Phenomenon in High Achieving Women: Dynamics and Therapeutic Intervention," *Psychotherapy: Theory, Research and Practice*, Vol.15, No.3, 1978.

17. Sandi Mann, *Why do I feel like an Imposter? How to understand and cope with Imposter Syndrome*, (London: Watkins Publishing, 2019).

18. Anxiety and Depression Association of America, "Facts and Statistics", Accessed: https://adaa.org/about-adaa/press-room/facts-statistics

19. Kyle Eschenroeder, "21 Proven Ways to Overcome Impostor Syndrome."

CHAPTER 10

THE SONG THAT
NEVER ENDS

WHY DO I do what I do? This is a question I ask myself all of the time. It's a question that can also be reflective. Why did I do what I did? That one can be a lot tougher, often taking me back in the healthiest of ways.

How would I enter the room that first day of my Sony internship now? What would I say differently? I would opt for the truth. I would aim for some sort of breadcrumb into what it really meant for me, a nobody, to be at a major record label as a junior. Music is my life. I play the drums. The artists on the label have written lyrics that I've scribbled in love letters. It was a dream to be there and all I wanted to do was learn the business side of an art form that I loved. Hindsight is 20/20 and passion plays out more dramatically in the mind, but even a fraction in that direction could have made a dramatic impact.

As the gap between our personal and professional lives diminishes, you and I are left to ask the question: what am I doing right now? Why am I doing this? To illustrate the miracle that put you in the position you are in will always be a story worth telling. We started by looking at what attracts us to good stories and their core elements. You are the hero. Sometimes you are the villain. In between, you are the treasurer, the analyst, the family member, and more. With each hat you put on and with every character you meet, you learn something new. These characters influence your behavior and your business regardless of where in life you encountered them. As you examined your life, you learned the biggest questions to ask. In this social science, the answers can and should evolve all in the name of staying in line with that elusive concept of authenticity.

We tapped into the power of claiming your story, understanding the sweet spot of truth and perception. Armed with not only the elements of good storytelling as an entrepreneur but also how to frame it, we took a pause and looked around. Where you are influences who you are. In a battle of nurture versus nature, the latter is a powerful force best recognized as such.

Finally, we took a step back and questioned all that we built. The hardest part of any endeavor is dealing with doubt. When we are winning, it's easy to believe our successes are a result of effort, but it is easy to wonder if our story tells more when fortune fails. To avoid vain complacency in our accomplishments and our work is to remain authentic in our life.

The importance of storytelling in business and the importance of being earnest continues to grow in a world where opportunities and pitfalls exponentially increase with technology. From marketing to sales and conversation to keynote, write your story and marvel at the unbelievable autobiography you are writing with every breath you are lucky enough to breathe.

ACKNOWLEDGMENTS

Thank you to Tina Wells for asking me to speak at Wharton. Without her kindness and willingness to open doors, this book would have never happened.